MW01100457

Dumb Money

Published by Mitchell Huynh, B.Sc., B.Comm., M.B.A.

All copy rights reserved.

Printed and distributed by Amazon.com

Dedication

To my loving parents, who have raised me and supported me to become whatever I want (doctor or dentist LoL), who now must settle for a business man;

To my beautiful wife, who must put up with my crazy ideas (or so they seemed until I make them happen);

To my loyal squad, who have journeyed with me from our breakdancing days, to now, our breaking the bank days;

To you, congrats on beginning your own journey.

Disclaimer: This is NOT an English literary novel. Expect grammar and spelling mistakes. As I tell my students, I'm not here to put an A on your transcript, I'm here to put several M's in your bank account.

"Let me be your guide from The Working Person to The Wealthy Person."

Introduction

I wasn't always the financial "genius" as I am often called these days. Mitch Millions, Money Mitch, Financial Ninja, Mitch Deezed are a few of my more common nicknames.

During university (I attended the University Of Toronto Mississauga, where I now teach among other things) and up until about 5 years ago, "the squad" and I were pursuing our dreams of becoming professional breakdancers and touring around the world. (Its true! You can Google us, type "GG Squad" and Much Music – yes, that's me falling on national television). We did this during university and even after we graduated while I was working as an advisor at Scotiabank. We still believed we would get there.

What we had, was a winner's mindset which we cultivated during our university days. Train hard; Put in the work; Be the best.

This book and where I am today in life, is the result of taking that same mindset and applying it in my daily life.

"If you knew better, you would do better." I take this saying everywhere I go. I came from the bank industry, where average people gave pretty much the same financial advice to everyone who walked in the door.

That's when I realized, to do better we must be more discerning about who is eligible to give us advice on "insert topic." If its finances, what have you done in your own life regarding finances that has set you apart from the average person? What have you done in your client's lives that set them apart from the average person? What have you done that was so amazing that I should listen to you?

There had to be something more, something out there that could impact people's financial lives in a more tangible way than what we currently had at the banks.

That realization made me pursue my MBA, in search of more. During my MBA, I had two epiphanies. First, my BHAG (Big Hairy Audacious Goal) was to touch the lives of 5,000,000 people in a positive way. Second, wealth inequality.

How could I combat wealth inequality? I originally created a start up, which paid our users $5.25/hour for using our phone or desktop application. We accomplished this by funneling ad revenues to our users (the people who watch at the ads). Thus, by giving people money for something they are already doing, I believed I was fighting wealth inequality. That was until we found out that one of the biggest tech companies out there at the rights to patent our ecosystem.

That start up experience was when I realized I could no longer work for anyone else. I needed to be my own boss.

I decided to join Investors Group and build my wealth management practice. Through educating both my clients and other consultants, I hoped to provide people the financial knowledge to succeed. This was a big gamble, as consulting at Investors Group is a 100% commission-based job, that means, if you don't sell, you don't eat. I was able to quickly become one of the top performing consultants from my first year there, by understanding what the financial industry lacked.

The first few months at Investors Group was TOUGH. I worked long hours, and built up my clients quickly, but my hard work wasn't reflected in my bank account. I studied how Investors Group compensation worked and quickly came to realize that I would need to sell to quite a few families and individuals to make a decent income OR I could sell to a few business owners and high net worth individuals. And so, that is what I did. I dove deep into how business owners run their businesses and what they need from the financial industry. It came down to tax efficiencies and strategies to create tax free income over the long term. Surprisingly, very few individuals specialized in this space, primarily top tax lawyers on Bay St. in Toronto who charge upwards of $1000/hour for advice. I learned everything about this niche area of financial planning and began to offer my knowledge as a value add to my business owner and high net worth clients.

I quickly came to realize that everyone could be using these same strategies, except no one was teaching them as there was so much more money to be made in the High Net worth market.

I couldn't reach enough people working at Investors Group. That's when I decided to have my own personal finance TV shows. The conversation with my fiancée at the time went like this.

Me: "Baby! Wouldn't it be awesome if I had my own TV show?!"

Cherie: "Yes, would be really cool but it's probably very difficult to get your own show."

I tuned out the 2nd half of her sentence, because I was too busy envisioning my show. Instead of one, I got two! One on Rogers TV which I called Smart Money, and one on Cogeco TV called Finance My Life.

I quickly moved up to the role of Director in only 18 months with Investors Group (the fastest move to Director in the company – see the Negotiations section for how I pulled this off).

I still wasn't satisfied with the impact I was making. My next crazy idea was to become a professor teaching personal finance at the top higher education institution in Canada – none other than my alma mater, The University of Toronto.

The conversation with my fiancée went like this:

Me: "Hey baby! What do you think of me becoming a Prof at U of T?!"

Cherie: "Why are you copying me?" (back story – she is an elementary school teacher at the Toronto District School Board)

Me: "LoL kk"

And so, I designed the course curriculum, contacted a friend I had working in the Management Department at that time to pitch the idea. They did a quick survey to assess demand and found that quite a few students would be interested in taking it. Armed with that information, I sat down with the director of the Management Department to discuss.

And here we are 2 years later, with each semester me teaching 150 students for a total of 300 students per year! Hopefully there is a trickle-down effect and my students teach their parents and loved ones.

Shortly after getting the position at UTM, I stepped down from my role of Director at Investors Group as I found it restricting for both myself and my clients. For my clients, I could only offer Power Financial products as Power Financial Corp was the mother company of Investors Group which also owned Canada Life, Great West Life, Mackenzie Investments, Putnam Investments, Wealth Simple etc. For myself, Investors Group greatly discourages any outside activity other than working for them. As you will read later in the book, you want to not only diversify your investments, but also, your income.

I moved into the role of Director at Experior Financial Group. A dynamic new financial management firm with great training and leadership. My knowledge allowed me to garner the respect of the leadership and I became the "Go To" person for the High Net worth and Business Owner clientele of the firm (read How to become the key person section) as well as build a strong team of active advisors across Canada.

This allowed me the flexibility to go to the office when I wanted, only needing to see my clients and submit business.

This was pivotal, as I was able to generate more than a six-figure income on part-time hours, thus allowing me to build my real estate portfolio, other lines of business, and of course my human capital.

There are so many opportunities out there that we miss every single day. Opportunities to build our cash flow, net worth, human capital etc. These opportunities are in front of us every day all the time. However, because we are so busy and focused on working for our "bosses" and the responsibilities of every day lives, our brain has been trained to ignore these opportunities.

There is always so much going on around us (lights, sounds, movements). Our brain has been trained to cut out things that are not important. If our brain was to analyze and dissect all these stimuli, we would go crazy.

Our brain is trained to only react to things that we tell it are important. Everything else, it will tend to ignore. You will notice this when you buy a new car. Before you got the car, it was a unique good-looking car. After you got the car, everyone seems to have one. That's because now, your brain is trained to recognize the car because it is important to you.

That's the same with opportunities. This book will teach you what is out there and how to use it, as I have. Once you tell your brain to start looking for these things, suddenly, they will be everywhere for you to pick and choose. Combine that with being a key-person and the results will be endless!

With these new opportunities will come new challenges. Don't be afraid to take them head on. As a species, we have evolved to survive. One way to survive is to preserve energy. Brain activity consumes a lot of energy. You will notice this during days in which you may not have done much physically, but you were mentally and emotionally stressed out and at the end of that day, your body was also totally drained.

Through evolution, we have evolved to be lazy and preserve energy by limiting our brain power. We are naturally lazy. If given the chance, we will more likely than not pick the easier path. The path of least resistance. Our brain is the same. If you believe that there is no solution to something, your brain will automatically shut down and stop thinking about that issue.

Our brain is fascinating and powerful. But it is only as strong as you are. Our brain doesn't know what is true or untrue. Therefore, if you tell your brain something is doable, your brain will automatically try to figure out a solution. Trust me, there is a solution to everything – but not if you've told your brain to give up! You will notice this, when you bump into someone you haven't seen in a long time. You've forgotten their name, but deep down, you know without a doubt that you know their name. A day, or maybe a week later, their name will pop into your head. That's the power of your brain believing there is a solution. It will continue working on the issue subconsciously without you noticing.

Don't be afraid to take on new opportunities, because you will figure out a way to execute successfully. Believe that you can, and you will.

A far-fetched dream of mine was to build a "GG (that's the name of my squad) Compound", which would be a private neighbourhood in which the entire squad and our families would live. This was something I thought about 10 years ago. Today, among other things I am a condo developer, developing a 12 story, 345-unit condo in Toronto. Building that GG Compound is not such a far-fetched dream after all!

Our conversation went like this:

Me: "Hey baby! What if I build condos?"

Cherie: "You build something? roflroflroflmao"

(backstory – I am the least handy person I know, don't call me to help assemble IKEA furniture!)

How in the world did I go from a financial advisor, to a TV show host, to a university professor, to a director of a wealth management firm, to owning multiple rental properties in Toronto, to a condo developer in Toronto in 4 years all at the same time? Unyielding belief in myself.

I now have built a real estate portfolio worth well over 8 figures in the Toronto area (and that's not even my full-time job!). I like to say I have many part time jobs (which I do, see all the above and add full time husband and doggy daddy to two dogs with our first baby on the way).

The key to building multiple sources of income, is having all your sources of income build on each other. Each one of my "side hustles" are related to each other. Therefore, as I develop one of them, all the others increase in value as well. So, by spending 1 hour working on one of them, I am actually producing 5 hours of benefit (assuming I have 5 part-time side hustles).

This is the same concept involved in our financial planning and wealth building. You never want to use one dollar as one dollar. You always want to find a way to use that same one dollar to do several things. If you can, you've effectively created several dollars from that one dollar.

Sir Isaac Newton said it best "If I have seen further it is only by standing on the shoulders of giants." Now, I am no giant, as I am still on my way to the goal of $100M, which I should reach in 10 years if I continue to move at this pace.

I do hope after reading this book and applying the concepts you've learned you will achieve similar if not greater success than I have.

Dedicate yourself to reading this book and understanding the concepts. I promise you the rewards will be limitless. The beginning portion of the book will be a bit dry, but persevere, trust me. I need to take you back to square one, to build up your mind so that it can more effectively absorb the later sections of the book.

"Banks are the Walmarts and McDonalds of the financial industry"

Section 1: The Banking Industry

Why do we need to understand banking?

Because banking is how the world goes 'round. Banks are where we put our money.   Chequings accounts, savings accounts, investment accounts – they are all held at some sort of bank or financial institution. We need to understand how banks work and how banks make profit so we can understand why we receive certain pieces of advice from the banks and the government. The government regulate the banks, the banks regulate our finances.

Banks are great starting points for our financial growth. That's because they are the intermediary where we receive and pay money from. Banks are on every single corner of every block, just like McDonalds and Walmarts. Eating at McDonalds is definitely convenient, but it isn't exactly great for our health. We can probably live entirely off the offerings at McDonalds, but if your goal is to be in peak physical health – this probably won't help. Shopping at Walmart is great on the wallet, you can buy a lot of average products for low prices – but these every day average products won't change your life. It's the same with the banks. What the banks offer is the average financial solution for the everyday person. If we don't want to be the everyday person, if we want more, we need to do things differently than the everyday person. The way you can guarantee that you will be average, is to follow and emulate the average person. If that is what you are looking for, then stop reading right now. The information in this book will take you far beyond your wildest dreams if executed properly, and because of that, it will seem unbelievable and unachievable. If you want to discover how you can exponentially increase your net worth and your cashflow beyond that of the average person – keep reading and take notes.

Banking started back in the day, when people were carrying around heavy pieces of gold. It came to a point, where people no longer wanted to carry around these heavy pieces of gold. Someone came up with the idea where they said, give me your gold, and I will give you a piece of paper saying you have this much gold. That was how banking began. The bankers now wanted to increase their profits. How would they be able to do that? By lending out the gold they already store in their vaults from their current clients. This is how fractional banking was born. Simply put, the banks would lend out a majority share of the gold held in their vaults, and retain a fraction for liquidity (i.e. In case a client came by asking to withdraw their gold). The borrower would receive a certificate (i.e. A slip of paper) with an amount of gold on it and would then in turn pay the bank some interest for the borrowed amount of gold. As you can see, one piece of gold can multiple many times over, creating a huge volume of money flow.

This creates a problem, as sometimes when countries can't pay back their debts and are going bankrupt (see Italy several years ago) and their citizens all run to the banks to withdraw their money, the banks don't have enough money to give everyone. In those cases, the banks limit the amount of money their customers can withdraw per day to ensure that all customers can be served.

See below for a quick example of fractional banking. Pretend Mr. A deposits $100, if the fractional banking requirement is 10%, the bank will then turn around and lend out $90 to Mr. B (10% of $100 is $10, therefore, the bank only needs to keep $10 of that $100). Mr. B then deposits that $90, into his bank account. The bank then will lend out $81, which is 90% of Mr. B's $90 deposit. So on and so forth. If we continue this several times, the banks have turned a $100 deposit into almost $1000 of cash flow in the economy.

You deposit $100	Bank loans $90 to someone else
That person deposits $90	Bank loans $81 to someone else
That person deposits $81	Bank loans $72 to someone else
That person deposits $72	Bank loans $65 to someone else
That person deposits $65	Bank loans $59 to someone else
That person deposits $59	Bank loans $53 to someone else
That person deposits $53	Bank loans $47 to someone else
Total Credit Notes: $520	**Total Deposits: $467**

Today, rather than a credit note, we just log into our bank accounts online, on our phones or laptop, and we will see a balance there. We can easily see how fractional banking puts more money into the economy then there actually is.

Accounts:

When we walk into the bank, we encounter a variety of accounts:

i)   Chequings
ii)   Savings
iii)   RRSP
iv)   TFSA
v)   RESP
vi)   Non-registered savings/investment account

We've already identified one way how banks make profit, that is interest from lending money to their clients. Another large profit maker of the banks is fees. Banks are gradually looking to increase the fees they can charge on their services as this is a more reliable form of revenue since interest rates fluctuate while fees are fully in their control. A lot of bank accounts have a fee attached to them.

Chequings

The chequing/checking account is a transactional account – meaning it is a daily use account where your direct deposits come in to (i.e. Your biweekly pay) and automatic payments (mortgage payments, car payments, cellphone bill etc.) come out of. This is not an account which you use to save money.

There are several different types of chequing accounts offered at the banks. Bank account fees are usually dependent on the number of transactions they allow you to do in a month before charging an additional service fee per transaction. It's good to note that banks don't care how many times you deposit money (credits), they only care about the number of withdrawals (debits). When we say transactions, we mean debit transactions which are withdrawals.

This is important to us, because if we go over the number of included transactions (at the bank they call them "free" transactions – but we know better than to think of them as free), we will be paying around $1.00 per additional transaction. In general, the higher usage the bank allows us to have without charging additional fees, the higher the monthly fee for the account.

It doesn't sound like a lot, but that mean that every time an automatic bill is paid from the account, or we "tap" our debit card at the store and we are over our monthly transaction limit, we are paying an additional $1.00. This adds up during the course of a month. I've seen people pay an extra $30-$50 per month for several months because they didn't understand how fees were charged on their account. Keep in mind your purchase habits and how you use your account to make sure the account you have is the right one for your lifestyle. Make sure you avoid paying unnecessary fees.

Types of chequing accounts:

1) There is usually a free youth and student account that offers a limited number of debit transactions (withdrawals of any kind).

2) A basic account with a few transactions (8 – 12). The monthly fees are within the range of $3-5 dollars, which is waived if you keep a balance of $1000-2000 in the account for each and every day of the month.

3) A medium usage account with more transactions (20-25). The monthly fees are within the range of $8-10, which is waived if you keep a balance of $3000+ in the account for each and every day of the month.

4) A high usage (unlimited) account. The monthly fees are within the range of $12-15, which is waived if you keep a balance of $5000 in the account for each and every day of the month.

5) A seniors account which offers a discounted or free unlimited account. Senior accounts usually start at age 58-60 depending on the bank. Make sure you ask for them to switch you to a seniors account if you qualify.

If you notice, there is a common trend with the accounts. The higher number of included transactions, the higher the monthly fees, and the more money we need to keep in the account to qualify for our fees to be waived. If you want the monthly fee waiver, you can't have your account balance fall below the required amount even by 1 cent for the entire month, or you will need to pay the monthly fee.

As long as you keep the minimum balance in the account for the entire month, the monthly fee is waived by the bank, as they are now able to lend on the balance in your account making up the loss of the account fee through interest.

Savings Account

Another very common type of account at the bank. Don't be fooled by the name of the account, as you won't receive much in terms of interest or savings benefits by using this account. This account is mainly used for organizational purposes, for you to separate your daily usage money (in the chequing account) and short term money (under 1 year) you need for a certain goal.

This is a non-transactional account, which means you shouldn't be withdrawing money from this account regularly. The banks discourage this, by charging $5.00 each for every withdrawal over the monthly limit (it ranges between 0-2 withdrawals). In general, you will want to do an online or mobile transfer from your savings account into your chequings account if you want access to the money (and then withdraw from your chequings account).

There are a few different types of savings account. For the most part, they offer very little in terms of interest (0-1.25% annually), and you need to keep a minimum amount of $5000 in the account to qualify for the higher range of interest. To put that in context for you, if you kept $5000 in there for an entire year, you would receive $62.50 at the end of the year (or $5.21 per month).

Generally, we use this account for organizational purposes - separating our money into different buckets for short term goals.

RRSP

This is one of the more popular types of investment accounts offered at the banks. RRSP stands for Registered Retirement Savings Plan. This is an account created by the government to help us save for retirement (hence the name). The theory behind this account is that to incentivize us to save for retirement, when we contribute money each year to our RRSP account, the government will return the extra income tax they took from us during the year (which was automatically deducted from our pay by our employers) in the form of a tax rebate. So every year once you do your taxes, in May or June the government will send you your tax return in the form of a cheque or a direct deposit. And since the government is returning our taxes to us today, when we withdraw from our RRSPs later on (in retirement lets say), at that point we will need to pay income tax on the withdrawal.

The RRSP account contribution limit depends on the amount of income you made last year. Currently the limits are the lower of 18% of the previous year's income OR the lesser of $26,500 (as of 2019). That means if you made $100,000 last year, you can contribute up to (by contribute, we mean deposit into your RRSP account) $18,000 this year. If you made $200,000 last year, you can only contribute up to $26,500 this year. Unused RRSP contribution room from previous years accumulate year over year. You have up to the end of February of the next year to contribute. For example, your 2018 RRSP contributions can be made up until March 1st of 2019.

Your tax rebate is based on your marginal tax bracket. Marginal meaning that for every extra dollar you make you make, how much of that is going to taxes. For example, if for every additional dollar you made, $0.40 went to taxes, then your marginal tax bracket would be 40%. Therefore, in our previous example, if you made $100,000 last year (2018) and you contributed $18,000 this year (in Feb 2019) your tax rebate would be $6,579 (making your average tax bracket around 37%). This is because your employer will automatically deduct income tax from your pay for the government. This means, at the end of the year, your employer will have deducted income tax based on an income of $100,000. By contributing $18,000 to your RRSP, the government considers your income to be only $82,000 rather than $100,000 (that is $100,000 income - $18,000 contribution = $82,000), and returns the extra tax your employer paid on your behalf in the form of a tax rebate.

All financial institutions should offer a feeless RRSP account which you can open and own personally. Since these accounts are linked to your personal taxes, these accounts must be owned solely – meaning only by you, therefore you cannot have a joint RRSP account.

Spousal RRSP accounts allow you to contribute to an RRSP account owned by your spouse. This means when your spouse withdraws the funds, it will be taxed in their name. This will allow you to split up your taxable income (later when your spouse withdraws) and reduces your taxable income today. For example, if your household requires $60,000 gross to live, then you can withdraw $30,000/year, and your spouse can withdraw $30,000/year vs. you withdrawing the full $60,000. If you lived in Ontario – your household would pay a total of $7,340 between you and your spouse, as compared to $11,025 if one of you withdrew the full $60,000. Your personal RRSP contribution limit still applies whether or not you are contributing to your RRSP or a spousal RRSP account, which means the RRSP deduction and tax credit will be based on your tax bracket.

Another popular form of RRSP account is the Group RRSP. If you are fortunate enough that your company offers a group RRSP account which they do contribution matching (an example of matching is if you contribute $1.00 to the group RRSP, your employer will contribute $0.50 on your behalf. This is a 50% matching) MAX THAT OUT! Most employers will cap the group RRSP contribution at a percentage of your income. But it is FREE MONEY, so take it. One of the few times I would contribute to an RRSP, is if I am receiving FREE MONEY! Your contributions and your employer's contributions will lower your RRSP contribution limit. If your limit was $18,000, and combined you and your employer contributed $3,000 to your group RRSP, then the maximum amount you could contribute to your sole RRSP would be $15,000.

This entire RRSP model is based on the assumption that while you are working, your marginal income tax is higher, than when you are retired. Contrary to this belief, most people actually spend more money in retirement than in their working years. This is because we've worked our whole lives to now enjoy ourselves; and if we've worked hard enough and invested our money wisely, we don't want to retire on a slim budget to avoid income taxes (when we withdraw our money to pay for retirement). As we advance in our careers, it's only natural that our lifestyle grows as well. We will have larger homes, drive nicer cars, eat out at fancy restaurants, and buy more things as our incomes grow. The minute we retire, we aren't going to go from eating steak and lobster to living off of mac' and cheese (although mac and cheese is delicious). We want to maintain the lifestyle we have earned and grown to enjoy in retirement. That means, we will be using at least as much money in retirement as we did while working.

On top of that, as we grow older, our health will deteriorate, increasing our medical expenses. If that wasn't enough, inflation will eat away at our purchasing power. Meaning, every year with the same dollar, we can buy less and less due to a slow increase in prices of our day to day needs. This means in retirement, we will most likely end up spending more money, than when we were working. This means, in retirement, if we listened to the media and the banks and invested as much money as we could into our RRSPs, we would be paying MORE in income tax to the government than if we hadn't invested in RRSPs in the first place.

If you run the numbers, you will see that RRSPs are literally a tax grab by the government. Essentially, it's an account that will give you a bit back today, and take a lot from you tomorrow. (Something to keep in mind, our economy is largely run by income taxes. When people retire, they will no longer pay income tax. So how does the government ensure that an entire population of older people continue to pay income tax until they die? Create an RRSP account and offer it at all the financial institutions.)

That being said however, there is 1 instance in which the RRSP account works in our favour. That's the First Time Home Buyers Plan (HBP). The RRSP account has only 2 ways in which you can access your funds tax-free. One of them, is the HBP. The HBP is a program the government put in place to help us buy our first real estate property. It allows you to BORROW up to $35,000 from your RRSP (which you would have needed to contribute to your RRSP account first, and then you can borrow it for the HBP) for each person on title. (Being on title to the home, means you own a portion of the house relative to your amount on title. 100% title, means you own 100% of the house. In marriage, normally both spouses are on title 50-50). This means if you are buying a home with your spouse/significant other/partner/business partner, you each can borrow up to $35,000 from your RRSP tax-free for a total of $70,000 to put towards your first home purchase.

The main condition to qualify for the HBP is that you cannot have been on title for any property for the last 5 years and the funds need to be in your RRSP account for at least 90 days. The caveat to the HBP is that you will "need" to (I recommend you don't) return the funds to your RRSP account over the next 15 years. That means if you borrowed $35,000 from your RRSP account you will need to repay $2,333.33 to your account each year for the next 15 years (or $194.44 per month). If you do as we recommend, and you don't repay the funds, then $2,333.33 will be added to your income for the next 15 years and you will need to pay a bit more income tax for the next 15 years. As an example, if your marginal rate rate is 30%, that means on $2,333.33 extra income you will need to pay an extra $700 in taxes a year (30% x $2,333.33) or $58.33 per month. I believe it is better to NOT repay the funds, FIRSTLY as I outlined above – the RRSP account will force you to pay a lot more in taxes later on compared to the small tax rebate you will receive today. SECONDLY, cash flow wise you are better off NOT repaying. If you were to repay, you would need to repay $2,333.33 a year, compared to not repaying and paying a bit more extra tax of $700 a year. Which means at the end of the day, you would have $1633.33 extra cash per year to go towards other more tax efficient investments. This means that you will be a lot better off in the long run by not repaying the HBP loan.

The other time you can access the money from your RRSP tax-free is through another program called "Life Long Learning Plan" (LLP). It is similar to the HBP in that you need to borrow the funds from your RRSP and repay it over TEN years. This program allows you to borrow up to $10,000 per year up to a maximum of $20,000 total from your RRSP account for education at a qualified institution (college or university) for continuing education. Once again, we recommend you do NOT repay the loan and avoid the RRSP account as much as possible for the reasons stated above.

TFSA

The Tax Free Savings Account (TFSA) is my favorite account. Primarily because, it is tax free! That means, all the money you make from your investments in the TFSA account, when you withdraw it, is tax free dollar for dollar. That is amazing! This is the ONLY registered account which allows you to do so. Planning wise this is extremely important as many government benefits (CPP – Canadian Pension Plan), and work place pensions we qualify for when we are older and getting ready to retire are taxable. This means, the more taxable income sources we have (withdrawals from our RRSPs being another one) the more taxes we will pay in retirement. Having a higher taxable income not only forces us to pay more in income taxes in retirement, but it also disqualifies us for the government benefits we have been contributing to throughout our working career – primarily our OAS (Old age security) benefits. Once our taxable income exceeds approximately $75,000/year, the government begins to claw back (pay us less OAS benefit) our benefits. Therefore, it is beneficial for us to focus on tax free income sources today, to prevent any type of claw back on government benefits later on. Other things we can't control 10-15 years from now, are the taxes we will have to pay.

One thing we do know for sure, is that the government is running out of money. (Interesting note: The CPP program was created when the average life expectancy was 70-72 years old. This means, the government planned on paying us CPP benefits from age 65 to age 72 – a total of 7 years of benefits. Today, a great majority of the population is living well into their 90s – meaning the

25

government is paying an additional 20 years of benefits which they did not budget for, and the program cannot sustain. You can see signs of the government running out of money as they offer "incentives" for people to delay claiming their CPP benefits at age 65 to age 70). Which means income taxes will either stay the same, but may most likely rise 15 years from today. In any sort of planning, you want to control everything you can, and not worry about things out of your control - things like government policies, income tax rates, government benefits etc. If we plan on depending on these things, our financial plan will have a high probability of going to shit. So let's not plan on depending on the government for our financial well being. To do so, we need to focus on non-taxable income sources, one of which is the TFSA account.

Since this account is so powerful in controlling our income tax brackets later on in life, obviously, there is a limit of how much money you can contribute. This program began in 2008, and each year the government gives us contribution amount which accumulates year after year if we don't use it.

Year	Contribution Limit	Cumulative Limit
2009-2012	$5,000	$20,000
2013-2014	$5,500	$31,000
2015	$10,000	$41,000
2016-2018	$5,500	$57,500
2019	$6,000	$63,500

The TFSA has a few key differences from the RRSP account which will allow you to maximize the amount of tax free money you can generate. One of these differences, is that after a withdrawal, that TFSA amount can be re-contributed the year after. For example, if you withdraw $1,000 from your TFSA, you can return that $1,000 the year after, along with the new increased contribution amount.

26

Understanding this principle will allow you to "lock-in" or "crystallize" the gains in your TFSA as additional contribution room.

For example, pretend that at the beginning of last year (2018, when the total contribution limit was $57,500) you contributed $5,000 to your TFSA account. You made a few good investment decisions, and your $5,000 grew to $8,000. The market goes up and down all the time. You being a smart investor realize this, so you withdraw $3,000 from your TFSA at the end of 2018 (the amount of gains you made). The next year (January 1st of every year), 2019, your contribution room grows from $57,500 to $63,500 (since every year the government allows an additional yearly contribution limit) PLUS $3,000 which you withdrew in 2018. Therefore your cumulative TFSA limit is now $66,500 instead of $63,500. By repeating this every year over and over again, your total contribution room will be far greater than the average person. Meaning your potential for higher tax free income later on is far greater than the next person. If you are reading this book, that is definitely what you will have.

TFSA vs RRSP summary:

	Tax Refund?	Taxed on Withdrawal?	Contribution Limit Reset?
RRSP	Yes	Yes	No
TFSA	No	No	Yes

RESP

This is a specialized account in which the government gives you FREE MONEY towards the post-secondary education of your child(ren) in Canada! That's right. Free. Money. You already know how I feel about free money. GET IT! Free money is the best money.

How the RESP works is that the government will match 20% of your contributions up to a maximum of $500 per year on your first $2500 per year of contributions to a maximum of $7200 of lifetime grant money (total grant accumulated over the entire lifetime). That means, you can deposit up to $2500 per year or $208 per month for 15 years to max out the government grant – this works out to a total of $36,000 in deposits per child. Any additional contributions will result in ZERO additional grant money. Therefore, anything on top of $2500 per year, or $208 per month is useless to you. There are other more efficient ways to save for your child's education outside of the RESP (Participating Whole Life policies being one of them – more on that in the later sections).

Withdrawals can be made when your child attends a qualifying institution (there is a list of qualifying institutions – most colleges and universities are on the list). The withdrawals will be taxed in your child's name. Most of the time, when our kids are attending university or college, they may be working part-time or not at all – therefore their tax brackets will be relatively low (or zero). Something to note: the personal tax exemption limit in Canada is $11,809 (as of 2019), which means anyone making LESS than $11,810 will pay $0 in income tax. Therefore, your child can withdraw up to that amount from their RESP account and pay no income tax. This is great, since funds inside the RESP grow tax deferred until the withdrawal. As long as the withdrawals plus your child's income is under $11,810 the RESP account CAN theoretically operate as a TFSA for your child's education.

One thing to look out for about the RESP account is that you can ONLY withdraw funds for EDUCATION (in a Canadian institution). This means, if your child decides not to pursue continuing education for whatever reason (going to a university in the States, becoming an entrepreneur, dropping out after 2nd year etc.) you may lose the funds inside of the RESP account. To avoid this i) do not over contribute, ii) the 20% Free Money is called the CESG

(Canada Education Savings Grant) – withdraw this money and the growth on this money first, when your child attends university or college. Withdrawing the government money is called EAP (education assistance payment). This money is ONLY accessible through education. Therefore, you want to use ALL of this money while you can. Later on, if your child decides not to pursue further education, you can withdraw the funds you contributed personally and the growth on that can be transferred to your RRSP. Your funds are called PSE (Post Secondary Education Payments). Your money remains your money, however, the government grants and growth on that can only be used for education.

Non-Registered Savings/Investment Account

This is an account used for general investments. Investments in this account do not grow tax deferred – whereas in the other registered accounts (RRSP, TFSA, RESP) the growth is tax deferred. That means every year you will need to declare investment income from your gains and pay taxes on the funds in this account. Most people use Non-registered accounts after they have maxed out their TFSAs and RRSPs (if they choose to use them).

NOTE: In all of the investment accounts (TFSA, RRSP, RESP, Non-Registered Accounts), you can invest the funds in multiple different asset classes. Imagine these accounts as a house, inside of this house there are multiple rooms (kitchen, dining, washroom, bedrooms etc) – each room has a different purpose (asset class). Therefore in 1 room, you can leave funds in cash, in another room you can invest in a GIC, in another room you can invest in Mutual Funds/ETFs etc. (more on different investment types in the later sections).

"Debt Builds Wealth"

SECTION 2: Credit & Debt

Understanding how credit and debt works will be ESSENTIAL to your financial health. A common misconception in the financial industry is that debt is bad. That's what they want you to believe. The truth is that Debt Creates Wealth.

Think about every single country, every single successful company – are they debt free? Or do they use debt to create more opportunities? It's the latter. If every single successful country, company, and individual uses debt to create cash flow opportunities – why are the banks and the media teaching us to stay away from debt?

Understanding how to use debt properly was one of the reasons I was able to build my networth from negative eighty thousand (-$80,000 CAD) after graduating from my MBA to several million CAD in under 5 years. Currently, I control over ten million dollars ($10,000,000 CAD) in real estate assets.

Networth (we will get into this later on) is taking the assets you own and subtracting all of your debt. If all you owned was a one million dollar house ($1,000,000 CAD) and you owed eight hundred thousand ($800,000 CAD) then your networth would be two hundred thousand ($200,000 CAD). If I continue on this path using the techniques I speak about in this book, my networth will reach one HUNDRED million ($100,000,000 CAD) in 10 years.

Whatever your financial goals may be, understanding this section will be the foundation of building your dreams. Don't hesitate to cover this section or any of the others multiple times as needed.

Credit Score

Your credit score is a numeric value which, simply put, tells everyone how responsible and how trustworthy you are financially. The higher your score, the higher the probability that you will repay your debts on time and vice versa. Scores tend to vary between 300 and 900 points. Most of the major banks will not lend you money unless your score is above 630 or 650. It is advisable that you maintain a score around 700 at a minimum.

It is far easier to maintain a good score than to rebuild a poor score.

The higher your score, the more debt you can responsibly take on since your score is a direct measure of how you manage your money in terms of debt repayment. The amount of debt you can take on is called your Total Debt Service Ratio (TDSR). This is a ratio of your income compared to your monthly payments. Therefore, the higher your income or the lower your monthly payments, the more new debt you can carry.

The formula the banks will use to determine if they will lend you new debt (TDSR):

$$TDSR = \frac{\text{Monthly Mortgage Payments + Property Taxes (Or Rent) + All Other Debt Payments}}{\text{Gross Monthly Income}}$$

The higher your credit score, the higher this ratio can be. However, in general banks will not allow you to go above 0.43. (This means 43% of your gross income is used to repay your monthly debt obligations).

When building and maintaining our credit score, we need to be aware of things that can negatively impact our score. These things are i) Late or missed payments, ii) Too many (or too few) open credit accounts, iii) High credit card and/or loan balances, iv) too many credit applications in a short period of time.

Late or missed payments will be reported on our credit report, and will hurt our score. Intuitively, if you are consistently late, or constantly miss payments, then it would be common sense that you are not responsible enough to take on new credit.

Too many open credit accounts will affect the amount of new debt you can carry, as it is a function of income. Everyone's income can carry only so much debt, therefore, if you already have borrowed as much as you can, your TDSR will not allow you to take on any new debt. Too few open credit accounts will result in a weak credit history as there hasn't been much activity on your credit report. You will want to have a few credit products (2 or 3 credit cards etc) that you use every month, and pay off every month to build up your credit history. You will need to prove you can carry larger amounts of debt if you want to apply for a mortgage (or any large loan). To do so, you will need to have an extensive credit history.

High credit card and/or loan balances point towards a shortage of cash flow. The credit system assumes that the only reason that you would ever use a large majority of your credit limit (limit is the amount available on your credit facility, ie. A limit of $1000 on your credit card) is that you are experiencing a cash flow shortage. This will negatively impact your score. Therefore, if you can avoid it, never use more than 75% of your credit limit. If your credit cards have a limit of $1000 each, then don't use over $750 on any card before paying it off.

Too many credit applications in a short period of time also imply an excessive need for funds, which points to a cash flow shortage. Every credit application will reduce your credit score by 10 points. Therefore, if your credit score is lower (ie. 630) a 10 point drop will affect you more than if you had a higher score (ie. 800).

Ensure you have a strong credit score from the very beginning. Make sure you keep up to date on bill payments. A lot of times you can schedule your bill payments using your online banking or you can allow your service providers to make an automatic withdrawal from your account (not recommended – as sometimes they may over charge you or continue charging you after you have discontinued the service with them).

Try not to hold a balance on your credit products (credit cards, lines of credit etc). Try your utmost to pay your credit card balances in full every single month. If you can't, make sure you make at least the minimum payment, and make multiple payments in the same month to the same product. This tricks the credit system into thinking that every time you have money, you are focusing on paying off your debt.

Always pay off your higher interest products first. These are usually your credit cards, then your lines of credit. Another trick is that if you have a lower interest rate line of credit (LOC) and a higher interest credit card, you can use your lower rate line of credit to pay off your high interest credit card. For example, if your credit card interest is 28% annually, and your line of credit is 6% annually, by using your LOC to pay off your $5000 credit card you are saving 22% in interest cost (28% - 6% = 22%) which works out to be $1,100 over an entire year. As a bonus, not only are you saving on interest, paying your credit card using your LOC also counts as a debt payment which will help boost up your credit score!

There are a lot of free services out there that will allow you to check your credit score for free. Creditkarma.ca is one, and a lot of banks allow you to monitor your credit using their online banking platform – completely free!

The Credit Application Process

It is important to know what to expect when you will be applying for debt. That way you can be fully prepared and have your documentation ready. This makes your banker's job easier, meaning it will be easier for you to get debt.

The first thing you will need is two (2) forms of identification. The most popular being i) Drivers Licence, ii) SIN (Social Insurance Number) Card, iii) Citizenship card, iv) Passport.

When applying for credit, your SIN needs to be one of your identifications as your SIN is directly linked to your credit score.

The next, is income verification. As we discussed above, any new debt amount is dependent on your ability to repay it, which means, income is necessary.

2 forms of income verification are needed.

If you are a salaried employee, you will need i) last two (2) pay stubs, ii) a recent job letter (stating your position as full-time, part-time, seasonal etc, rate of pay, and whether or not you are on probation, printed on a company letterhead). These items are usually easily obtained from your online employee portal and the job letter from your HR (Human resources) department.

If you are self employed, you will need to provide i) T1 generals for the last 2 years, ii) statement of business income (part of your T1s), iii) Notice of Assessments (NOAs for yourself personally, and/or from the business as applicable), iv) business bank statements for the last year (if applicable).

For self employed individuals, the banks like to see documents for the last 2 years to show that the business is stable and/or growing which means the loan they are about to give you is relatively safe.

Any credit application will require your legal consent as it is illegal for any institution to check your credit without your written or verbal authorization.

Credit Products:

Credit cards (CC)

Credit cards are one of the most popular and convenient forms of credit. As their name, it is in the form of a card, making it easily accessible and widely accepted by vendors. Credit cards are a form of revolving credit facility. That means, you can use them, pay them off, and use them again – hence revolving. They have a 21 day interest cycle. What that means to you, is that you can make a purchase using the card, and pay no interest for 21 days. Therefore, you have an interest free loan for just under a month. The catch is that if you don't pay the card off in full, then you will be charged a high amount of interest. In the world of debt, credit cards generally have the highest interest on average ranging from 19.99 – 28.99% annually.

There are a variety of credit cards out there offered by many companies. Visa, Mastercard, American Express to name a few. And within these card companies are many card offerings. The cards try to differentiate themselves by offering different types of reward points. Whatever it is you are interested in, there is probably a card out there for you. Rewards range from cash back, to travel, to merchandise. These reward cards range from free cards to cards with annual premiums. The higher the annual premium, the greater the rewards. You can generally work out if paying the fees is worth it for the additional rewards by calculating the monetary value of the additional rewards versus the total of what you would earn from the free rewards card plus the annual fees.

Occasionally, if you cannot get an unsecured credit card from the banks due to poor credit, no credit history, or a lack of income – you can request a secured credit card. This means you will need to lock away a sum of money with the bank before they will issue you a credit card. Usually the amount you lock away will need to be 120% of the credit limit. Therefore, if you want a $1000 credit card, you'll need to lock away $1200 in the bank. When you've built up enough credit history, a high enough credit score and enough income, you can re-apply for an unsecured card, and if you qualify, the bank will unlock and return your funds to you.

Examples of cards:

- Student: Usually no fee and has some form of cash back (0.25% - 1%)

- Low Interest: Interest anywhere from 6%-11%. Lower interest option may have fees.

- Cash back: Cash rebates on purchases (1%-4%). Higher end cards have annual fees.

- Travel and/or Other Rewards: Reward points may be redeemed for travel (or other rewards). 1 Point – 4 points per dollar spent. Higher end cards have annual fees.

- General Ranking of Cards:

    - Generic color, Silver, Gold, Black

Lines of Credit (LOC)

Lines of credit are another form of revolving debt facility. In general, LOCs are much lower interest than CC's and usually offer a much higher credit limit. LOCs limits usually start at $5,000, whereas CC's limits start at $500.

The primary difference between a LOC and a CC is that LOCs are not attached to a physical card like a CC is. To access your LOC, you can transfer funds via your online banking from your LOC to your chequing account and/or your CC (if you are making a payment to your CC as discussed above). You can also access your LOC at the ATM or the teller. Before online banking and phone apps, LOCs were far less convenient that the CC, but now that online transfers are so easy to do, the LOC can effectively act as a CC at a much lower interest rate. The two things the LOC lacks are the rewards, and 21 day interest free grace period that CC's offer as interest on the LOC is effective immediately. Therefore, LOCs are usually used when you plan on keeping a balance (ie. when you can't pay off the entire balance). By using the LOC to do this instead of the CC, you will save a ton of interest cost (as in the previous example).

Lines of Credit can be unsecured or secured. The difference is interest rate. Interest rates may be floating or fixed. Floating means that the interest rate moves according to the Prime Rate (P, the bank lending rate). Currently (Summer 2019) the Prime rate is 3.95%. Therefore, if your LOC interest rate is P + 4, your annual interest rate will be 7.95% (3.95% + 4%). If it is a fixed interest rate, then it stays consistent regardless of how P moves. Unsecured LOCs have a higher interest rate, usually around P + 2% to P + 7% depending on your credit score. Secured LOCs have a much lower interest rate. Usually secured LOCs are secured against real estate and generally have an interest rate of P to P + 1%.

A lot of times, financial institutions will give you an unsecured LOC without verifying your income if it is a student LOC and you are attending or about to attend an accredited program with high income potential (ie. Medical School, Dental School, MBA, Law etc). They will give you quite a generous amount (sometimes up to $50,000 plus). The payments on your LOC will be interest only until you graduate. To prove you are a current student you will need to show tuition paid and/or your course schedule. It is always better to have extra credit for any opportunities that may come up, than to run out of money during school and/or miss these opportunities. To maximize your credit, what you need to do is apply for a student LOC at all the banks on the same day. Remember in the previous section regarding credit score, the maximum amount of debt someone can take on depends on credit score and income. By applying at all the banks on the same day you bypass this requirement because the credit report system doesn't update that fast. Therefore, you will be approved for multiple LOCs before an update will be made on your credit report. This means that instead of having one LOC for $50,000, you will have as many as you want. Remember – use this strategy responsibly. You will still be responsible to pay back all the money you borrowed during your post grad education. However, it's better to have the ability to jump onto opportunities than to be forced to miss out because you didn't have the funds. These opportunities will be discussed in the Alternative Investments section.

Examples of LOC:

- Student LOC – generally issued for post-grad study options (MBA, Law school, Med School, certain Masters/PhD degrees)

- Home LOC – secured against real estate (interest rate: P to P + 1)

- Unsecured LOC – general LOC (interest rate 8.99%)

Fixed Term Loans

Fix term loans are as they sound. They are a non-revolving credit facility – meaning that as you pay them down, the limit doesn't return like a LOC or a CC. The good thing about fixed term loans are that the interest rate is constant for the length of the loan. They are a great way to pay down debt and get rid of any debt you don't want. You can repay your loan in a variety of fixed installments either monthly, bi-weekly (26 payments a year), semi-monthly (24 payments a year, every 1st and 15th, or every 15th and 30th) or weekly for the term of the loan. By the end of the loan, your balance will be $0. The term can be several months to several years depending on the loan.

- Examples:

    - Secured: Car loan, Mortgage

    - Can also be unsecured – usually you can fix a portion of the LOC, and keep a portion revolving

Mortgages

Mortgages and secured LOCs are by far my favorite type of credit product. These have the lowest interest cost of all the lending products. Cheap debt is a means to create wealth if you use it properly. We will get into how you can use cheap debt to increase your cash flow and your income, which will increase the amount of cheap debt you can carry, which will increase your cash flow and your income – rinse and repeat. Properly using cheap debt will accelerate the building of your networth more than you can imagine. We will discuss this in further detail in the later sections.

Mortgages are a non-revolving credit facility used to purchase a property. The property is usually amortized over 25 to 30 years. This means that if the interest rate and the mortgage payments stay the same for the next 25 years, then at the end of 25 years (the amortization period) your mortgage will be completely paid off. (Remember, we never really want to pay off our mortgages, as this is the cheapest source of debt).

When purchasing a residential property, ideally if your income is strong enough you want to put down (your down payment amount) as little as possible, keeping as much of your money as liquid as possible. In the world of finance, liquid means your money is not locked up. However, there are minimum down payment requirements we need to follow depending on your purchase price.

On homes under $1,000,000 CAD, you need to put down 5% on the first $499,999.99; 10% on the balance from $500,000.00 to $999,999.99 CAD.

If your purchase price is $1,000,000 or higher, your minimum down payment is 20% on the entire purchase price.

Example:

> Home value: $999,999
>
> Minimum down payment = 5% of the first $500,000 + 10% of the remaining balance
>
>> = 5% x $500,000 + 10% x $499,999
>>
>> = $25,000 + $49,999.90
>>
>> = $74,999.90

However, if the home purchase price was $1M, the min DP would be $200,000.

This is where negotiations come in, if you can reduce your purchase price to below $1,000,000.00 that makes a huge difference. Imagine needing to save $200,000 compared to $75,000 – how much longer would that take you.

There are many types of mortgage lenders in the industry. They are typically ranked from A-lenders, B-lenders, and then private lenders. A-lenders generally include all of the major banks, TD Bank, RBC, Scotiabank, Bank of Montreal, and CIBC to name a few. A-lenders are the most strict of all the lenders in terms of credit score and income requirements. B-lenders are a bit more lenient. Most medium sized lenders fall under the B-lender category. A few examples are Home Trust, Equitable Bank, and MCAP. Private lenders are the most lenient of all the lenders. Private lenders are "gray" market lenders who lend money for interest income. They generally do not emphasize credit score or income, but rather lend against the amount of equity you have in your home. Equity is the amount of home you actually own. To calculate this, take the market value of the property subtract the mortgage amount, and the difference is your equity. For example, if you have a $500,000 property, and you have a $350,000 mortgage, then your equity is $150,000 (which is $500,000 - $350,000 = $150,000). More on private lenders and how to become a private lender in later sections.

There are 2 main types of mortgages, Conventional mortgages and Collateral Mortgages. Within conventional and collateral, are open, fixed, and variable mortgages.

For conventional mortgages, only the actual amount of the mortgage loan is registered against your property. (What this means, is that for the bank to lend you a mortgage, they will register a lien against your property. This protects the bank's loan to you. This insures that if you were to sell your house, your lawyer would first, return the balance of the unpaid mortgage to the bank and then the rest would go to you as the home owner - the amount of your equity. If the bank didn't register a lien, then you could easily sell your property and take all the money and run.) Conventional mortgages are less convenient if you plan on re-borrowing money from your house relative to collateral mortgages.

Collateral mortgages are ones in which the bank registers the full house value as a lien. This facilitates easier re-borrowing (known as re-financing) of funds from the bank as you pay down your mortgage. Generally, the bank will allow you to re-finance up to 80% of your property's value (dependent on your income of course). Your property value will increase every year, generally at an average of 4-7% as long as you are in a suburban area in Canada, if you are in a major city you may even have 10%+ appreciation a year. Every time you re-finance a larger amount, the bank will need to register a new (and larger) lien amount against your property. Therefore, if a larger lien is already registered against your property, the bank can skip this step saving you time and legal fees.

Example:

Property Value $500,000. Down payment $100,000 (20%). Therefore, your mortgage balance is $400,000.

A Conventional Mortgage, the bank would register a $400,000 lien on your property.

A Collateral Mortgage, the bank would register a $500,000 lien on your property.

Which means, in 5 years when your property value grows from $500,000 to $575,000 and you want to borrow 80% of the value. You request to refinance for $460,000. With a conventional mortgage, the bank will have to redo all of the legal documents to register a new lien of $460,000 costing you time and fees. Alternatively, with a collateral mortgage, the bank already registered a $500,000 lien on your property, therefore lending you $460,000 is not an issue. No new legals or fees will be incurred.

The new mortgage of $460,000 is first used to pay off your old mortgage balance of $400,000 (lets assume), and the remaining $60,000 can be deposited into your account as cash. (Which you can use for whatever you want – ideally, some type of investment or another real estate down payment).

Although some banks like to differentiate themselves as offering Conventional mortgages or Collateral mortgages, the majority of banks have collateral mortgages as it makes life easier for everyone (unless your goal is to be mortgage free, in which case you will want a conventional mortgage. Note: I do not advise being mortgage free as a financial goal, because cheap debt is a powerful wealth building tool. As much as you may want to, its hard to eat bricks for dinner).

Lenders will generally lend up to 80% Loan to Value (LTV) on a property. For example, if the property value is $1,000,000 an 80%

LTV will give you an $800,000 mortgage. The other 20% is your down payment, which is the amount of equity you need to contribute to the home purchase. When you buy a property, on top of saving for the down payment there are other costs lumped into "closing costs." Closing costs include, land transfer tax, legal fees, movers etc. You will want to budget an extra 3-5% for closing costs.

If you can't put together 20% for a down payment (most people don't – also, I do not recommend it, as the more money you put into your house as a down payment, the less money you have to for other investments and opportunities), then you'll be applying for a High Ratio Mortgage (a mortgage with a LTV of higher than 80%). In theory, if your income can support it, you can put as little as 5% down on your primary residence. A primary residence is a property in which you will be living. Since your mortgage amount is a higher LTV, it is also riskier. Therefore, the bank will need your mortgage to be insured by a third party mortgage insurance company. The bank, which is doing your mortgage will apply with a mortgage insurance company on your behalf. Some of these providers are Genworth, CMHC, and Canada Guaranty. These companies insure that if you default (meaning if you cannot pay your mortgage for whatever reason), they will cover your payments for some time.

The insurance premium will be added to your total mortgage amount, however, you will be responsible for paying the HST upfront on closing.

90.1 - 95% financing	4.00%
85.1 - 90% financing	3.10%

80.1 - 85% financing	2.80%
Self_Employed (Purchase up to 95% LTV)	4.50%

There are a few types of mortgages banks offer. Most of them are Closed Mortgages. An Open Mortgage is a mortgage in which you can pay out (normally using another bank's mortgage) at any time without any penalty fees. Remember, banks make money through you paying interest – therefore, if they give you the option of leaving them, they will need to charge you a higher interest rate to make up for that income loss on their side, and that added flexibility and freedom on your side. Generally open mortgages will charge you around 6.0-6.5% interest.

Closed mortgages are your typical mortgage. Closed mortgages are either i) Variable or, ii) Fixed rate mortgages. Closed mortgages are as they sound. The term is closed, meaning that if you break your mortgage (by paying it out, or selling your property etc) there will be a penalty for doing so as the bank is trying to make up the profit they are losing from your interest payments for an early payout.

Fixed rate mortgages are mortgages in which the interest rate is the same (fixed) for the entire term. Popular terms are 2, 3, 4, and 5 year mortgages. 1, 7, and 10 year mortgages also are offered, however, they aren't as popular.   Usually when your term is 6 months away from maturing, the bank will offer you a renewal. You will want to negotiate your renewal rate and shop it around at other banks and lenders. Fixed rates are usually a bit higher than variable rates. For example, your average 3 to 5 year mortgage rates are close to 2.80 to 3.10%.

A variable rate mortgage is a 5 year term mortgage in which the rate fluctuates on the Prime rate (P). Therefore, as P moves up or down depending on the Bank of Canada, your mortgage will move up and down accordingly. An example of a variable rate would be P − 0.3. This means, if the Prime rate is 2.95, and your rate is P − 0.3, then your mortgage rate today would be 2.65%. The variable rate is usually a bit cheaper than the current fixed rate. If you believe the interest rates will stay the same or move lower over the next 5 years, get a variable mortgage. If you believe that interest rates will move up, get a fixed mortgage. If you chose a variable rate, and the interest rate starts to move up, you always have the option to lock into the current fixed rate offered, for the balance of the term or longer. For example, if you have a variable mortgage, and you are 2 years into the 5 year term and you notice interest rates rising, you can lock into a currently offered fixed 3 year term mortgage, or longer.

Mortgage Payments

As mortgages are a fixed term loan, payments are made in similar fashion. Usually preauthorized withdrawals from your bank account, weekly, semi-monthly, bi-weekly, or monthly. The more installments you make towards your mortgage the faster you pay it down. This is because interest has less time to accrue. Therefore, by paying weekly, you pay the least amount of interest (all things being equal), and you make a few extra weekly payments therefore you pay off your mortgage sooner.

- Weekly = 52 payments (ie. every Monday)

- Semi-monthly = 24 payments (1st and 15th of every month)

- Bi-weekly = 26 payments (ie. every other Monday of the month)

- Monthly = 12 payments (ie. 1st of the month)

47

Re-financing

Re-financing is when a home owner re-mortgages (gets a new mortgage) their property, usually to free up cash when they've paid down a portion of their mortgage and/or when their property value has increased. Lenders will only allow you to re-finance up to an 80% LTV, usually using a collateral mortgage – subject to income (remember TDSR).

> Example: Home purchased in 2016 for $650,000. Current mortgage balance of $575,000. Home assessed in 2017 at $850,000. Home owner wishes to take some capital from the home for renos/investments/paying for "insert" expenses.

- Home owner is able to borrow up to 80% LTV of the home

    - New mortgage amount of $680,000.

    - After discharging (paying out) the previous mortgage the home owner is left with $680,000 - $575,000 = $105,000.00 (in their bank account)

The above example is a real example of the first property my wife, Cherie (my girlfriend at the time) and I bought. We put into the house a total of $75,000. We put down a slightly larger than a minimum down payment, as our incomes at the time couldn't support a large enough mortgage for a minimum down payment. This was my awakening regarding the power of real estate. We put into the house $75,000, and one year later, the house value went from $650,000 to $850,000. An increase of $200,000 in a ONE year period on an initial investment of $75,000. What is even better, is that this was a rental property which we received $2,500/month. Meaning, the house generated $30,000 in rental income a year. Therefore, in one year the house generated $230,000 on an initial investment of $75,000. That is a return of 300% ($230,000 / $75,000) in one year. That is AMAZING. That is the POWER of leverage and good debt. Even though we invested $75,000, the entire value of the house ($650,000) grows, not only the down payment. Your average mutual fund or market investment will only return about 5-8% a year on average. Therefore, if we invested the $75,000 in a mutual fund and made a whopping 10% on it, we would have a total of $82,500 at the end of the year ($75,000 x 0.10 = $7,500 plus the original principal of $75,000 = $82,500). This is a lot less than making over $200,000 in a year with a lot less risk.

It is funny how life throws you curve balls, which turn out to be blessings in disguise. The back story to this purchase, was that Cherie (who was my girlfriend at the time) and I were looking to move in together. Her family is a conservative Christian family, which meant we weren't supposed to be spending nights together before marriage. Even when we went away on vacation we would have to book a room with two beds in it (LoL). We've been dating now for about 5 years, and moving in together was the logical next step in the relationship. We started shopping for a house and put in a few offers, and finally, we won a bid on a property we liked. Cherie was so excited that we went out and ordered all the furniture so that when the house closed (that's when we take possession of the house and get the key), the furniture would arrive over the following days, and then it would be move-in ready. We went back to Cherie's parents house and told them we had bought a house and would be moving in together. And they pretty much said NOPE! At that point, I was thinking "Wtf? How are we going to have a fully furnished house, with regular mortgage payments and not live there together."

At that point, we decided to rent out the property rather than just one of us living there. That's when I learned my first two most important lessons in finance. 1) LEVERAGE (good debt) greatly increases your returns. 2) Your first property should be an investment property and/or rental property, NOT your primary residence. As your primary residence will never buy you your dream home, but your investment property will.

When you refinance your home, you can use any combination of mortgage, LOC, and credit cards (up to a maximum of 65% LTV on revolving credit products).

> Ie. In our last example:

- We are left with $105,000 we can use. If we take it all as part of a mortgage, the excess amount is deposited into our chequing account.

- However, we can take $55,000 as a mortgage (which translates to cash), and $50,000 as a secured LOC limit, and $5,000 as a new secured Visa. (Total limit is still $105,000 of new borrowing).

The following year, we got married and bought a house to move in together (finally!). We were able to fund our wedding (close to 75k all in) using the funds ($105,000) we re-financed out of the investment property and luckily we broke even on the wedding due to the generosity of cash gifts from our guests. This allowed us to put down a down payment on our new home. Our new home (which we currently live in and have for the last 2 years) was a large bungalow with a relatively large land size for the Toronto area. We bought this house with three intentions, firstly – we have 2 small dogs so an oversized backyard is great for running around and playing fetch; secondly – to rent out the fully renovated basement, which has a full kitchen, bathroom, and 4 large bedrooms; thirdly - to re-develop the area by combining our property and a few of our neighbours to build a small town house complex (more on how to re-develop property in the later sections). Any time you make a purchase, it needs to be smart. There needs to be more than a single use for it (ie. For my family to live in). The more options, the more value it has.

"Make your money work for you, so you don't have to work for your money."

Section 3: Investments

This portion is your basic introduction to investments. As Warren Buffet says, "Unless you can find a way to make money while you sleep, you will be working until you die." Working until we die isn't exactly the ideal situation – not for anyone, and especially not for you, which is why you are hear reading this book in the first place. You need to make your money work for you, so you don't have to work for your money.

This portion we will take you through the investments that are offered main stream, primarily through the banking institutions. You can imagine that if something is offered by the banks, everyone who banks there is probably using the same products, getting the same results, which means – you would be exactly in the same place as everyone else. When it comes to purchasing power, if everyone is able to purchase the same things, no one is better off than anyone else. This is going to increase inflation (be discussed below), which means everything increases slightly in price to match everyone's increased purchasing power. Therefore, the end result is that nothing changes for you, nothing changes for anyone else.

This is the exact reason why we cannot be doing what everyone else is. It is in our best interest to do things differently. We need to increase our purchasing power relative to everyone else. Any products and strategies offered main stream at the banks (which is available to everyone) is a good way to keep everyone on the same level.

Alternative investments and strategies which will take you far beyond anyone else, which I used to accelerate my finances, will be discussed in later sections. However, we need to understand what is out there and how it works, to fully appreciate how much better these alternative investments and strategies are.

Inflation

Inflation is one of the primary reasons why we need to invest and grow our money. It is rate at which the price of an average basket of goods increases year over year. If you think back to your childhood, any product you pick out will be quite a bit cheaper back then, than it is today. I remember when cans of pop (soda) from the vending machines were only $0.50, and now that exact can of pop is $1.25. That's a 150% increase in price. Therefore, when I was 5 years old and I had a dollar, I would be able to buy two cans of pop. If I saved that money under my mattress until today, I wouldn't be able to buy even one can of pop.

Currently as of summer 2019, rate of inflation is 1.4%. Between 1915 and 2017, the average yearly inflation has been 3.04%. Inflation historically had a high of 21.60% in 1920. If we had $100 in 1915, today that same $100 would need to grow to $2,271 for you to buy the same amount of things.

For your investment returns, you need to make MORE than the rate of inflation to grow your money. If your money stays the same (ie. $100 value this year, and $100 10 years from now), you are actually LOSING money because inflation is eating away at your purchase power. So we need to consider what does your investment pay, net of inflation.

In this section, we will be speaking about different main stream investment options - Cash/GICs, Bonds, Mutual Funds, Exchange Traded Funds (ETF), Segregated Funds, and Stocks.

Cash & GICS

Cash is exactly as it sounds. This is just money under your mattress, in a safety deposit box, in your chequing account, or your savings account. This doesn't do much for us. It won't grow, but if you need money quickly and easily it will be there waiting for you without any type of risk. If you put away $100 in cash, it will always be $100.

GIC stands for Guaranteed Investment Certificate. This is the safest investment vehicle you can have. There is very little risk to your money, but that also means, there is very little return. In general, the more risk, the more potential for higher returns. GICs don't offer high returns, but you can almost never lose money. Your money is locked into a fixed rate contract. Your funds are usually locked for a little as a few months to 5 or 10 years. The longer the term, the higher the returns. Your average GIC will give you a return in the range of 0.5%-2.25%. However, you won't be able to access and withdraw your funds until the end of the term (which is known as maturity). If you choose to break the contract, then you will not only lose whatever interest you've gained, but also a penalty fee. Therefore, before you lock in your funds – make sure you won't need it for the length of the term. What a GIC will do for you, is protect your purchasing power with no risk, as long as you can stay in the GIC for the entire term. Note, a GIC will never make you rich or wealthy.

Bonds

Bonds are a little higher risk than GICs but offer a high return, as your principal is relatively protected. A bond is you loaning your money to whoever (usually the government, or a company) and them paying you a rate of interest for it. Government bonds can pay anywhere from 3-12%, company bonds range between the same as well. The quality of the bond (translates into the trustworthiness of the borrower) is rated from AAA to C (Junk bonds). The higher the rating, the lower the interest. Your main risk is that the government or the company may default on the loan (be unable to make the loan payment and go bankrupt). If this happens, bonds (or any debt of that matter) are safer than shares (or any kind of equity). In terms of bankruptcy, debt holders are paid back first and if there is any money left over, then it goes towards repaying the shareholders.

Mutual Funds

Mutual Funds are a portfolio of bonds, stocks or other investable assets selected and managed by a professional team on behalf of investors. These funds are generally higher risk depending on the asset mix in the fund. There are a wide variety of funds. Whatever it is you are interested in, there is a fund for it - whether it is a specific industry, geographic region, or risk level. It is the portfolio team's responsibility to pick and choose the best assets to invest in, in that specific industry, geographical region, or risk level. Since these funds are managed by a team, there is a cost. This cost is called the Management Expense Ratio (MER). This expense goes towards paying the team for their work – this fee is paid regardless of whether you make money or not. The more actively managed the fund, the higher the MER. Usually the MER ranges between 1% to 2.7% and is paid automatically every year.

In terms of mutual fund fees, there are 2 main types of fees; i) Deferred Sales Charge (DSC), and ii) No Load (NL). For DSC funds, there is no upfront fee deducted when you invest and your MER is typical a bit lower. This is because these funds require you to stay invested for about 5 to 7 years. If you exit the DSC funds environment there will be a withdrawal fee. (You can switch between DSC funds with no fee). This fee can be quite expensive. In the first year, it can be as high as 5.5% which lowers each year until the 7th year. After the 7th year, there will be no withdrawal fee. For No Load funds, the yearly MER is higher since there is no withdrawal fee during any year. Therefore, for short term investments, NL funds are better. If you plan on staying invested for several years DSC funds are better. The breakeven point between the two types is around 4.5 years. Therefore, if you plan on investing under 4.5 years, pick the NL fund; if you plan on investing for longer than 4.5 years, pick the DSC fund. For every fund, there is a NL and a DSC option – so don't worry about missing out.

- Typical Fund categories: Dividend Income Fund, US Opportunities, Asia Fund, Gold Funds, Bond Funds etc.

Exchange Traded Funds (ETFs)

Exchange Traded Funds are funds which track an index, commodity or a basket of assets. They are similar to mutual funds in that there is an ETF for everything that there is a mutual fund for. The difference is that ETFs are passive investments. This means they are not managed. If you are investing in gold mining companies for example, and there are only 2 gold mining companies and company A is 80% of the industry and company B is 20% of the industry, the ETF must own 80% of company A, and 20% of company B in that same proportion in the fund. However, since there is very little in terms of decision making or research, ETFs have very low fees compared to mutual funds. The typical ETF fees are usually 0.25% to 1%.

There is a big debate in the investment world of banks (the world of average investors) of which is better, mutual funds or exchange traded funds. In an environment where the economy is expanding and the markets are going up, ETFs are generally better long term since the fees are much lower. In an environment where the economy is stagnant and the market is moving sideways, or if the economy is shrinking and the market is going down, mutual funds generally perform better even with their higher fees. This is mainly due to mutual funds being actively managed. Firstly, this means that the fund can have a certain portion held in cash, so the fund isn't fully exposed to the down turns in the market. For example, if your fund is 20% in cash, and 80% invested and the market is going down, than only 80% of your money invested in the fund is losing value and the rest of the money is sitting in cash waiting for an opportunity to buy into the market again. Secondly, in the example above if there are only 2 companies, A and B, the ETF will need to hold 80% of A, and 20% of B. If A is going bankrupt, the ETF would still need to hold 80% A and 20% B, meaning that you may potentially lose 80% of your funds invested. If this was a mutual fund, the portfolio management team could invest 90% into B and only 10% in A and you would lose only potentially 10% of your funds invested.

Therefore, it is advantageous for your long-term financial health to understand the limits and strengths of the investment vehicles you are investing in.

Stocks

Buying stocks, simply put, is picking and choosing to buy into and own a small piece of a company in hopes that the company's market value increases and/or the company pays you a dividend (a quarterly, semi annually, or annual payment proportional to a percentage of the share value). A share is one ownership piece of the company. When you are an owner of a company (share holder) you have voting rights and will be invited to the company's annual general shareholders meeting.

Buying stocks is generally higher risk than owning a mutual fund or an ETF as most mutual funds and ETFs own multiple companies according to their specific investment criteria, sometimes up to hundreds of different companies or assets within that category. Therefore, for a mutual fund or an ETF to go to zero is quite rare, whereas if you were to invest all your money into one company, its much easier for that one company to go to zero rather than hundreds of companies in that industry.

If you are interested in trading stocks and day trading – please visit my online course portal www.dumbmoney.ca. Day trading and stock picking course to launch end of 2019.

Investment Considerations

There are a few things you will need to consider when making investment decisions. Risk tolerance is one of the keys to making your investment decisions. This will play a key role in your decision making of when to buy and when to sell. Unfortunately, emotions play a big role in whether we make or lose money. How would you feel if you woke up one morning and your portfolio was down 10%, 20%, or 30%? What would you do at that point? Panic and sell, be paralyzed in shock, or get excited and buy more? The amount of money you can calmly lose, will decide what type of investment risk you can take.

Emotions

The market tends to be cyclical (see below), there are mountain peaks and valleys. The uninformed investor tends to get excited and jump in at the peaks – the areas of maximum greed, which results in maximum loss potential as now you are buying at the highs of the market. The uninformed investor tends to panic and sell their portfolio into cash at the valleys, the areas of maximum fear, which results in missing out on the quick recovery period as the market balances itself out.

One of the ways to prevent ourselves from panicking and selling at the very bottom, or experiencing FOMO (fear of missing out) and buying at the very top is to understand the big investment picture. The market over the long term is growing. This is due to technological advancements, allowing us to be more efficient in our daily lives, as well as live longer. Population increases by itself will grow an economy as there are more people therefore there will be more demand for products. If we look back historically, we have had short term catastrophic events – the great depression, Y2K crash, the subprime mortgage crisis of 2008 etc. Yet, all of these events are just a tiny blip on the markets as you can see below. Each one of these events was a short term down turn in the market, after which the market bounced back and continued to grow.

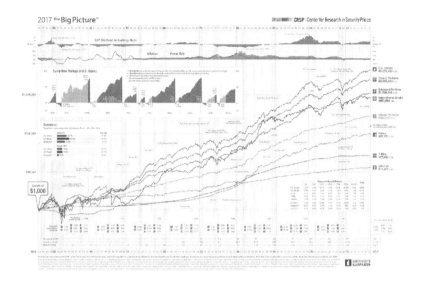

The above chart (known as an Andex chart) tracks different portfolios from 1925 until 2017, starting with an initial investment of $1000. If we had invested $1000 into a US focused stock portfolio (most risky) from 1925 until today, we would have over $5,200,000.00 today. If we invested in a balanced portfolio (a mixture of equity and income generating assets – medium risk), we would have over $1,200,000 today. If we only want to match inflation, we need to make sure our $1000 grows close to $14,000 today. As you can see, through every single crisis and market "crash", as long as you can wait for the market to recover and continue on its growth path, you will make money.

Therefore, not only is your risk tolerance important, but your investment timeline is just as important. The longer your timeline, the more risk you can take, as you have the luxury of waiting for the market to recovery and grow.

As your investment timeline shrinks and you need access to the funds, you should gradually move from more risk to less risk to prevent any market downturns from taking a chunk of your money just as you need it.

Diversification

Diversification is an important consideration when building a portfolio. Simply put, this means we want ensure our eggs are not all in one basket. We are able to do this by buying stocks in companies in different industries, different countries, different asset mixes. We can do this by hand picking stocks, mutual funds, or ETFs. You want to make sure that your mutual funds or ETFs do not overlap in their asset holdings. You can have 5 mutual funds from 5 different companies all invested in the same things – which means you are not diversified at all.

As a quick summary, when putting your portfolio together understand your risk tolerance, your investment timeline, and how diversified you are.

Taxation

Another thing you want to consider when putting together a portfolio, is not only your returns (gross returns), but what actually hits your bank account (your net returns). Different types of investments are taxed differently. So if you are investing outside of a tax deferred account, you need to understand how much you will actually make. What hits your bank account is what is going to change your life. What the returns are on paper is just that, paper. Nice to look at, nice to talk about but worthless, unless its in your bank account.

Type of returns on main stream investments are i) Capital gains, ii) Dividends, iii) Interest

Capital gains

Taxed on 50% of realized gains at marginal tax rate (some exceptions: primary residence, selling a business which will be covered in later sections). This is the most advantageous type of investment income in terms of taxes. A capital gain is you buying a mutual fund, etf, stock for $1.00 (book value) and it grows to $4.00 (market value). Therefore, your capital gain is $3.00 ($4.00 - $1.00). 50% of that $3.00 is tax-free ($1.50); 50% of that $3.00 ($1.50) is taxable at your marginal tax rate. If your marginal tax rate is 45%, then you would pay a total of $0.675 in taxes ($1.50 x 0.45 = $0.675). This works out to be about 22% in tax (the lower your marginal tax rate, the lower the capital gains tax you pay – the maximum tax you will pay on capital gains is approximately 25%).

Dividend gains

A dividend is a distribution from a company to reward their shareholders. Usually this comes from companies which are mature in their industries. Rather than keep the excess profits in the company, they are paying it out to their shareholders because they don't have as many opportunities to use those funds to grow the company (as they are matured). If the dividends are 5%, and the share price is $10.00, this means that as long as you own the share before their dividend distribution date (known as ex-dividend date) you will receive $0.50.

There are two types of dividend income i) Eligible (dividends from a publicly traded Canadian corporation), ii) Non-eligible (dividends from a non-Canadian corporation).

- Eligible (Public Canadian Corp) Tax: Simplified version: 1) Gross up dividend income by 38% and multiply by marginal tax rate (ie. 40%). 2) Grossed up dividend income multiplied by dividend tax credit of 25%. Then take 1) – 2).

- Dividends Eligible: Simplified version: 1) Gross up dividend income by 38% and multiply by marginal tax rate (40% - if you make around $92k/year). 2) Grossed up dividend income multiplied by dividend tax credit 25%. 1) – 2).

- Example: $70 in dividend income x Gross up (38%)

- Therefore $70 x 1.38 = $96.60

- $96.60 x 40% (marginal tax rate) = $38.64

- $96.60 x 25% (dividend tax credit) = $24.15

- $38.64 - $24.15 = $14.49 in taxes on $70 of eligible dividend income

- Approximately 21% in income taxes

- Dividends Non-eligible: Pay full dividend income at marginal tax rate plus withholding tax (which is 15% for US dividend stocks which can be reclaimed on line 405 of your tax return).

Interest Income

Interest income is taxed at your marginal tax rate – as simple as that. This is the highest taxed type of investment income. If you receive $100.00 in interest income, and your marginal tax rate is 45%. You will pay $45.00 in tax.

Investment Platforms

There are plenty of ways for you to get involved in investments. There are three main ways, i) Banks and Credit Unions, ii) Asset Managers, iii) Do It Yourself Platforms.

Banks and Credit Unions

One of the more popular ways is talking to your bank advisor and opening up one of the investment accounts we spoke about in the last section (RRSP, TFSA, Non-registered, RESP). Your bank advisor will have you fill out a risk tolerance and timeline questionnaire to determine what type of mutual funds and ETFs the advisor can put your money in. All of the banks and credit unions offer some type of mutual funds and/or ETFs for your investment accounts.

Asset Managers

These are private wealth management companies such Investors Group, Sunlife, Edward Jones, Experior etc. There are a host of different companies. Some of these companies have a limited product shelf whereas others have access to all the products on the market. Generally, the larger companies (Investors Group, Sunlife etc.) are limited to selling their sister companies' products.

These companies offer everything the banks do with some differences in terms of investment product shelf, and insurance offerings.

Do It Yourself Platforms

Most of your banks will have an online investment platform. For example, TD has Waterhouse, and Scotia has iTrade. There are private platforms as well, such as Quest Trade. These platforms allow you to buy and sell mutual funds, ETFs, and individual stocks. There is a fee for every buy and sell. For new accounts or if you hold enough assets, you may be eligible for a certain number of free trades and or a discounted fee.

I recommend that if you can take some time, always manage at least a small portion of your own funds. That way you force yourself to keep up with the markets and understand what is going on. No one is going to care about your money as much as you do.

Between the banks and private wealth advising companies, it is hard to say which is better. It really depends on your advisor. The quality, knowledge, and work ethic of advisors have quite a wide range within both segments. Ideally, you want to have an advisor who has shown a track record of doing what they say they can do – as shown either on their own finances and or for their clients. The worst thing you can do is entrust your hard-earned money to an advisor who has less or equal knowledge and experience as you do. Warren Buffett said it best, "Wall Street is the only place that people ride to in a Rolls Royce, to get advice from those who take the subway." This makes absolutely no sense, however, this is what the financial industry is built on. Your absolute trust in them, even though they have not earned it. Who in their right mind would hand over their hard earned money, and the financial well being of their family to someone they don't know with no verifiable track record. But that's how the industry works, and that's why the majority of the population are average and will stay average. Its because the advice and execution they receive is average. If you were running a company, would you hire anyone in any position unless you've interviewed them, examined their resume, and spoken to their references? Imagine hiring someone to do something as important as taking care of your company's bank account and finances without doing any research on them? Absolute madness. Do you want to manage my finances? Show me what you have done for yourself and your clients. I don't care if you've been working in the industry for 10 or 25 years. Why are you broke then? Why are your clients broke? Number of years in an industry or position doesn't equal an increasing knowledge or performance. It could quite possibly be that they don't have 25 years of experience; they actually only have 1 year of experience repeated 25 times.

"Success in life is the intersection of achievement and significance."

Section 4: Financial Planning

A financial plan takes a look at where you are today and where you want to go. It defines your short- and long-term financial goals and how you can reach them. For most people, financial planning is non-existent. Most of the time we spend whatever is in the bank account, and save whatever is left over. We need to be able to put together cash flows and balance sheets as businesses do. This is why businesses are able to make projections, track milestones, and pivot to make changes if those milestones are not achieved.

"Conflicting financial priorities and stressful choices are a 'fact of life' for Canadians — with 79% not confident they'll achieve their financial life goals" – *National Post*

"More than two thirds of Canadians worry 'a lot' about money, but 69% still don't have a plan" – *National Post*

A good financial plan will, i) identify your short-term and long-term goals, ii) take a detailed look at where you are today, iii) analyze your budget, iv) create measurable and time-based goals, v) review your financial standing annually.

In this section I will take you through how to put together a strong financial plan. I will run through an example so you can do it for yourself and your loved ones.

The goal of financial planning is to become wealthy. Wealthy means different things to different people. Essentially being wealthy means that tomorrow, you can stay home and never go to work another day in your life and not worry about money. Depending on how luxurious your lifestyle is, the amount of money you need to be wealthy will differ. Understanding your monthly expenses to upkeep your ideal lifestyle will be important in putting together your financial plan. Something to start thinking about now.

Wealth doesn't relate to money alone. Money won't make you completely satisfied with your life. Success in life is the intersection of achievement and significance. Achievement usually results in financial rewards while significance results in relational rewards of understanding that you've made a difference in someone's life. If you are able to gear your financial planning towards who you want to be, and what you want to achieve, you'll be able focus your time and money on what matters most to you. It sounds vague at first, but understanding the bigger picture will allow you to fill in the gaps on how to get there (more on becoming the key person in the later sections).

I'll give an example of my life to clear it up. Years ago when I first started dating my wife, she spoke about how she eventually wanted to move to Africa, open a school to teach local underprivileged kids, house the less fortunate, and live off of potatoes. In my mind I was thinking, "sure once we've done what we need to do, that sounds great except I can't live off of potatoes." A bit of a back story on Cherie – growing up she has always wanted to teacher and a mother, she loves children. She also loves helping others as she is a Christian by faith. I am currently a seeker and have been seeking for several years now. I'm obviously motivated by different things than she is. However, I saw her as a life partner back then and so I planned our financial strategy around teaching others (about wealth) and housing those who are in need. Today we have several rental properties in Toronto, and we work with The Toronto Homeless Shelters' Refugee program to house their refugees in our properties. Refugees come with a social stigma, very few landlords are willing to take them on. Partly, because landlords look for tenants with a strong credit history, and sustainable income to pay the rent. Therefore, it takes a lot of trust for a landlord to take on someone who is new to the country, with no job and no credit history. However, working alongside the refugees' case workers to house these individuals allows them to obtain a work permit and start contributing to the economy. Without a permanent residence, they would not be able to get a work permit. I'm proud to say several of our tenants have gotten full time jobs in industries ranging from construction to health care and are now moving towards being completely independent, contributing members of the economy.

How does this help us find the intersection between achievement and significance? Financially, we have built a comfortable real estate portfolio which pays us rental income. Financially, this makes sense as our tenants receive government benefits to cover their rent and some living expenses until they get on their feet. Through building a self-sustaining real estate portfolio, we find achievement. Relationship wise, we have strong relationships with our tenants. We guide and advise them through this transitional process of moving to a new country and starting all over again. Through participating in our tenants' lives we find significance.

Moving up the pyramid of wealth requires only three steps. These steps are 1) Work, 2) Save, 3) Invest. If you work, save, invest, work, save, invest, work, save, invest enough times, plan and execute properly you will get to wealthy.

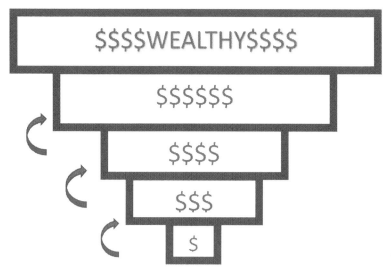

If you know that you can eventually get to wealthy as long as you can get through the steps enough times, then what you would want to do, is bullet-proof your plan to make sure you can repeat those steps. From the steps Work, Save, Invest the last two steps are impossible without the first. Therefore, as long as we can protect the first step "work," we can complete the last two steps "save and invest." Work, means anything we do that generates an income. In most cases, this means going to the office and working for your employer. Or it may be going to your own office and working for yourself.

The main threat to us not becoming wealthy is losing our ability to work, which is losing our ability to generate an income. If you receive a salary of $80,000.00 annually and you expect to work for the next 25 years, then your ability to work is worth $2,000,000.00 – and we want to protect this.

Insurances:

There are three main threats to our ability to earning this money i) getting sick, ii) getting injured, iii) dying early. If any of these threats materialize in our lives, particularly i) and ii), this means we won't be able to work and generate an income. Just because we don't have an income anymore, doesn't mean our bills will stop. Bills and expenses will keep on coming. To maintain our standard of living, we will start using our savings to pay these expenses, and once our savings are gone, we will start using our lines of credit and credit cards to cover the expenses. If this happens, instead of moving up the ladder to wealthy, you will be moving backwards. That means that you may never get to wealthy.

Good news is, we can hedge our risk and guarantee that if any or all of those three things happen to us, it won't affect our financial plan and we will get to wealthy. There are specialized insurances that protect us against this. Any time we do any sort of financial planning or risk hedging or investments we want to be able to use the same dollar to hit as many goals as possible. By doing so, we are able to "re-use" the same dollar multiple times, thereby effectively turning our one dollar into two or three. The way we will use insurances is not only to protect us from risk, but also, to build up our networth.

Critical Illness

Firstly, we want to protect ourselves against getting sick. Getting sick means being diagnosed with a critical illness and surviving for 30 days after the diagnosis. It is a under discussed area, as everyone without exception, believes they are healthy. However, statistics show that 1 in every 3 people will be diagnosed with cancer. A good friend of mine was diagnosed with cancer at the age of 36, and is currently undergoing treatment. Luckily for him,

74

it was caught early and as he is relatively young so his body is recovering quickly from the treatment. Critical illness (CI) insurance covers 25 of the most common conditions, these are: Heart attack, Alzheimer's disease, Bacterial meningitis, Coronary artery bypass, Heart valve replacement, Loss of limbs, Major organ failure on waiting list for transplant, Occupational HIV infection, Severe burns, Stroke, Aortic surgery, Benign brain tumour, Coma, Kidney failure, Loss of speech, Motor neuron disease, Paralysis, Cancer, Aplastic anaemia, Blindness, Deafness, Loss of independent existence*, Major organ transplant, Multiple sclerosis, Parkinson's disease. As you can see, the list is quite comprehensive, however, also check with your insurance provider what other conditions are offered on top of these.

This type of protection is for what happens IF we live (and hopefully we do). Getting a critical illness is not just something that will affect our own earning potential but our loved ones as well. As you go through the treatments and the recovery process, most likely it's not only you, but also your family, in particular, your spouse who will be there taking care of you through out this time. Therefore, it is at least two incomes we want to consider covering should we get a critical illness policy.

How the critical illness coverage works is that after you've survived your diagnosis for thirty days you will receive a cheque for the coverage amount tax free. The coverage amount is up to you, normally you will want to cover both incomes for at least one year. So if you make $55,000 annually and your spouse makes $55,000 annually, you will want to buy $110,000 of critical illness coverage. How you use the money is up to you as well, whether it is taking the family on a dream vacation to create memories, taking time off work for you and your spouse to focus on recovering, or paying for the highest level of medical treatment or all of the above.

Paying for you CI policy is the same as most insurances, you can pay a lump sum at the beginning of every year, or monthly. The cost of the policy depends on your age and your health as with most insurances.

However, we want this CI policy not only to protect your financial plan from any type of critical illness but also, we want it to build your wealth. All CI policies have an extra option (extra options for insurance policies are known as Riders) you will want to purchase called, the Return of Premium Rider. This rider will return all the money you've paid into the CI policy after a certain number of years. For most companies it is at the 15 year mark. With this rider, you have effectively turn your CI policy into a savings account. Let's say this policy costs $75 per month, therefore, over a 15 year period you've paid $13,500 ($75/month x 12 months/year x 15 years). The worst case scenario from the example above is, that your doctor diagnoses you with a critical illness, you survive for 30 days, and you get a cheque for $110,000 tax free. With this money, you and your spouse take a full year off to get you the best treatment, and to focus on your treatment and your recovery. You didn't need to take money out of your savings (RRSP, TFSA, other savings) to pay for your monthly living expenses while you were recovering. Therefore, even in the worst case scenario, you are still on track to becoming wealthy, even though you were got a critical illness.

The best case, is that you are healthy and in 15 years you decide that you don't need the CI policy anymore, so you cancel the policy and receive a cheque for $13,500 which you put towards anything you want (as this is now extra money coming back into your financial plan).

Disability Insurance

Secondly, we need to protect ourselves against getting injured. Whether it is mental stress or a car accident and we can no longer perform our regular jobs – disability insurance (DI) covers a variety of injuries. Getting a disability in any form will prevent us from doing our job, and therefore prevents us from generating an income.

DI policies will pay you a tax free monthly benefit of up to 66% of your gross monthly pay. The policies have a maximum monthly benefit which is slightly less than your regular monthly income to encourage you to heal and get back to work. If we can make just as much or more than our regular jobs using our DI policies, then no one would want to get better.

DI policies are a bit tricky as they have a few definitions we need to understand. DI policies categorizes your eligibility using three different definitions, i) own occupation, ii) regular occupation, iii) any occupation.

Own occupation is reserved for a certain category of jobs such as doctors, dentists. If you get disabled with OWN occupation, then you are able to quality for your full monthly benefits tax free, and get a new job at the same time without it affecting your benefits. For example, if you were a dentist and your hands shook, then you wouldn't be able to do your job. Therefore, your monthly benefits would kick in. In this real life example, this dentist's disability policy paid out $16,000/month tax free, and the dentist became a professor teaching dentistry at a university making a good income on top of that.

Regular occupation is the most common definition. If you get a disability, you will qualify for your monthly benefit tax free. However, if you get a job, then whatever income you make will reduce your disability benefit dollar for dollar. For example, if your monthly benefit is $5,000/month and you have a part-time job paying your $1,000/month, then your disability benefit would be reduced by $1,000 for a total benefit amount of $4,000 (instead of $5,000).

Any occupation is the worst definition. Any occupation means that if you can do ANY job, you don't qualify for anything. This means, if you can pick up the phone, you can work from home as a telemarketer.

Most work places have some sort of DI policy for their employees which cover up to a flat monthly maximum, usually between $1500 to $2500. Therefore, if you make a lot more than the maximum monthly benefit offered by your work place, you will need to look into topping up your coverage personally.

Something to look out for, is that most workplaces' DI policies have a Regular occupation definition, which drops to Any occupation after two years of benefits. If you only have a work place DI policy, make sure you get better in two years.

In terms of coverages, you want to own your own policies, because you have full control of them. If your employer decides to change things, lay your off, go bankrupt, all of that will affect your coverages, which affects you getting to wealthy.

As with everything, we want your DI policy to build your wealth. Like CI, DI also has a Return of Premium rider; some riders will return 100% of your money, some riders will return 50% of your money every 6 to 7 years. Once again, turning your DI policy into a savings account.

For DI policies, you want the policy to end at the age of retirement (normally at age 65). That's because the DI policy is there to protect your monthly income. Once you retire, there is no more monthly income to protect so you can cancel the policy at that point and get your return of premium.

Life Insurance:

The last thing we want to protect against, is early death. To do this, we need to look at Life insurance. There are a two main types of life insurance, i) term insurance, ii) permanent insurance.

Term Insurance

Term insurance is as it sounds. It only covers you for a specific term, after which it expires. If you die within the term of the insurance, the insurance will pay out a tax free death benefit. This type of insurance is the cheapest, as it is temporary. This means it is quite useful when a) you don't have a lot of cash flow, and b) when you have a temporary risk to manage.

When you have low cash flow but are looking to protect yourself and your family, most people look at term insurance. Usual terms are 5, 10, 15, 20, 30, and 100 years. At the end of the term, the insurance contract automatically renews at a much higher monthly premium. For example, for a $1,000,000 death benefit for a male, age 35, with average health will cost approximately $45/month for a 10 year term. At the end of the 10 year term, when it renews, the new monthly premium is now $270/month. You can imagine how much the premium will be 10 years after that, and another 10 years after that (its $660/month, and then $1879/month after that).

This type of insurance won't do much for you unless you die. It doesn't provide much value, it won't build your wealth. It is quite similar to renting an apartment. You don't own anything, and the minute you stop paying your monthly rent, you have no home. If you want to continue to rent, the monthly rent will increase every several years.

When we do financial planning, we want to focus not only on what if we die, but also, and most importantly, what happens if we live. If we live, we want to be wealthy. Luckily for us, permanent life insurance, known as Whole life, is one of the best ways to do so. Whole life is one of the financial industry's most well kept secrets in building wealth in a tax efficient manner. I use it, my clients use it and long term there are very few things that can compare if you use it correctly.

Whole Life Insurance:

There are two types of Whole life insurance. The first is Universal Whole Life, the second and my favorite, is Participating Whole Life.

Whole life insurance combines the best of both worlds; life insurance and tax free wealth building. Whole life gives you a Death Benefit, as well as an investment portion known as your Cash Surrender Value (CSV). When you die, the entire policy pays out tax free. If you live, that's when the magic happens. Most of these policies you can contribute and pay the premium from 8 to 20 years, after which you don't need to pay the premium anymore and the policy carries itself. This is known as a paid up policy. Your CSV grows tax deferred, and if you position it properly, you can access the money in it tax free. The key to being wealthy, is managing how much tax you pay, when you no longer work.

Universal Whole Life

During the time period in which you pay into the policy, your monthly premium is split into two parts, i) the life insurance, and ii) the other additional (optional) part goes toward funding the CSV. The additional monies grow tax free within the policy in the Cash Surrender Value (CSV). Within the CSV account you can invest the monies in a variety of offerings from the insurance company – GICS, Bonds, Mutual Funds etc. These monies can be used to i) offset and or paydown future premiums, ii) build your investment account which you can access at any time.

In terms of accessing the funds, there are two ways you can do it. Firstly, a straight withdrawal – there will be tax implications on the withdrawal. Secondly, the smarter way, is leveraging the money out. This means, you are borrowing against the value of the CSV. For Universal whole life, your LTV (loan to value) will range from 40% - 70% of the CSV value. This is because funds in the CSV in a Universal Whole Life on average are a lot more risky, because they are market dependent. Since it is a secured loan in the form of a Line of Credit (LOC), the interest rate should be lower than the average rate of return on your investments in the CSV. Since the money you will be using is on a LOC, you have access to money today tax free, while the funds will continue to grow in your CSV.

Participating Whole Life (PAR)

Participating whole life policies have the additional contribution amount built into the monthly premium. This money grows your CSV in a different way. Whereas the Universal policy allows you to decide what investments you invest in, the Participating pays you a portion of the insurance company's profits in the form of a tax free dividend. The tax free dividend is broken into a guaranteed dividend and a non-guaranteed portion. The guaranteed portion is contractually guaranteed to be paid every single year, where the non-guaranteed portion is optional. However, these insurance companies haven't missed a dividend payment in over 50 years. The dividend is a function of Portfolio returns which is highly co-related with Interest rates, Operational Costs, and Mortality rates (Company profits). Interest rates are at an all time low, therefore when we look long term, there is a high probability that interest rates will rise between now and your death. In terms of Operational Cost and Mortality Rates, there is usually a bonus that come from these, as companies will generally over estimate operational costs and mortality rates in their budgets compared to the actual costs. This is why companies are able to pay out such high returns consistently. Current dividend scales range from 5.25% to 6.50% depending on the company.

One of the key differences between Participating Whole Life is that the returns do not depend on the market as Universal Whole Life does. The returns are fairly consistent as you can see below. During the mortgage crisis of 2008, the S&P 500 (the top 500 companies in the US) Index LOST 33.00%, while the Par policy paid out 7.71%. That is a 7.71% GAIN compared to a 33.00% LOSS – which is a relative gain of 40% from the Par policy. Therefore, Participating Whole life can be used as a safe, consistent investment fund. Most high networth families use Par as a tax free shelter.

	Year	Par Dividend	S&P 500			Inflation
	2000	8.71	7.41	5.96	5.34	3.20
9/11 This event reduced consumer and investor confidence. The uncertain economic climate and large scale layoffs reduced consumer demand for goods and services. The Bank of Canada continued to lower interest rates into early 2002 to help restore consumer and investor confidence.	2001	8.96	-12.57	5.32	4.05	0.72
	2002	8.96	-12.44	5.08	3.91	3.80
	2003	8.61	26.72	4.54	3.13	2.08
	2004	7.86	14.48	4.34	2.92	2.13
	2005	7.46	24.13	3.89	2.71	2.09
	2006	7.46	17.26	4.18	3.16	1.67
	2007	7.71	9.83	4.25	3.31	2.38
	2008	7.71	-33.00	3.36	3.01	1.16
Recession	2009	7.71	35.05	2.84	1.95	1.32
	2010	7.36	17.61	2.88	1.97	2.35
	2011	7.36	-8.71	2.47	1.87	2.30
	2012	6.96	7.19	1.63	1.65	0.83
	2013	6.50	12.99	1.99	1.63	1.24
	2014	6.50	10.50	1.90	1.90	1.50
	2015	6.50	-8.32	1.19	1.47	1.61
	2016	6.00				

Another advantage of the Par policy, is that when you leverage your CSV for a secured Line Of Credit (the smart way of accessing the money in the CSV), the LTV is 90%. This is because the returns on the Par policy are not market dependent. This is a big difference between 90% LTV on a Par policy compared to Universal Whole Life which allows an LTV of only 40% - 70%. For a numerical example, if you had a CSV of $1,000,000 – a Par Policy would allow you access to $900,000 while a Universal may only allow you access to $400,000. That is a lot of money you are missing out on.

You would use this LOC to fund your retirement, whatever your monthly expenses are most of it would be paid from your LOC, whether it be $3,000 per month or $10,000 per month. Once you've used up your LOC, most likely it would be 10 to 15 years later, you can re-financing and leverage 90% of the new CSV amount (likely to at least double by this time). As long as you budget properly, your Par Policy essentially becomes a money tree. When you die, the policy pays out the Death Benefit, which pays off the LOC, and the remainder goes to your beneficiaries tax free. To see how effective PAR policies are, refer to the example in the Financial Planning for Entrepreneurs section.

Mortgage Insurance

This type of lender's insurance is quite popular as it is offered at every bank for every mortgage, line of credit, and credit card. This is the worst type of insurance there is on the market primarily because of 3 reasons. Firstly, you don't own it and your loved ones are not the beneficiaries. You pay for the insurance, however, the bank owns it, and the bank is the beneficiary. You and your loved ones have no choice in what the funds are used for. The funds can ONLY be used to pay back the bank loan. Remember, having options is key in determining your financial well being.

Secondly, (this applies more to mortgage loans) you have a decreasing benefit. This means, you pay the same monthly premium, however, year after year, your mortgage balance decreases as you pay it down. Therefore if you die, the amount that the insurance will pay off decreases every single year, while you continue to pay the same monthly premium.

Thirdly, the insurance is NOT underwritten at the time you apply for and purchase it. That means, you are not approved for the insurance that you are paying for. The underwriting happens at time of claim (when you die). Industry statistics show that 50% of all mortgage insurance policies at the bank level are NOT paid, most commonly due to a mistake made during the application. This means, you expected that your mortgage would be paid off when you died thus protecting your loved ones, but instead, the insurance was declined after your death resulting in no insurance pay out, and now your family will have to continue paying the costs of the mortgage without you around. If they cannot, they may have to sell the family home and up root their lives. This is not something you want your family to go through, particularly since they are still grieving for your passing. What happens instead of the bank paying off your mortgage, is they just return the amount of money you paid for the premiums. For example, your mortgage insurance may cost $75 per month, and you've paid it for 10 years. This means you've paid a total of $9,000 ($75 x 12 months x 10 years). Instead of paying off your mortgage of $500,000 – the bank instead returns the $9,000 to you. That's a HUGE difference in the quality of life for you family.

Mortgage insurance isn't really your best choice, especially when you can buy term or permanent insurance for the same monthly premium that you own and control.

Quick Comparison between Lender Insurance and Personal Insurance:

Lender Mortgage Life Insurance Plan	Personal Life Insurance Plan
Lender is the owner of the policy.	You own the policy and designate the beneficiary.
Pays benefits to the lender.	Pays benefits directly to your designated beneficiary.
Coverage expires when the mortgage is paid off.	Coverage continues after the mortgage is paid.
Pays out only the amount owing on the mortgage at the time of claim. Total value of coverage decreases with mortgage balance.	Pays the total life insurance coverage amount and the total coverage remains stable for the coverage period.
Premiums can be adjusted by the lender at any time.	Premium schedule is guaranteed for the life of the plan.
Lender can change or cancel the policy at any time.	Only you can cancel or make changes to the plan when premiums are kept up to date.
Policy cannot be moved to a new mortgage, a renewal or a new lender.	Plan goes with you from one home to another, one mortgage to the next.
Your premiums are based on your age and minimal health information. At time of claim, accuracy of answers to medical questions may	Your premiums are based on your age, health and smoking status.

"Plan like your life depends on it, because it does."

Section 4: Financial Planning

Financial Planning 1: The Snap Shot

The primary objective of a financial plan is to take a look at your personal finances as a proper business would look that theirs, with the goal of increasing your Net Worth year over year. Net worth is what you are worth financially. The calculation for this is take everything you own (at market value, what you can sell it for fairly) and subtract everything you owe (mortgages, lines of credit, credit cards, personal loans etc). The leftover, is your net worth. Net worth will be an important factor when you go to the banks for a loan. The higher your net worth, the easier and larger a loan you can get. The key is increasing your cash flow, and taking your cash flow to drive growth of net worth. Plan like your life depends on it, because it does.

The first thing we want to do, is to assess where we are today. This is known as a financial snapshot. To do so, we need to put together our balance sheet and cash flow. These terms are used often in accounting and finance and may sound complicated, but they are quite simple to put together.

Balance sheet, is everything you own minus everything you owe. This determines Net Worth and overall financial health.

Cash Flow is what comes in every month (all income) minus what goes out every month (all expenses). Determines how much you can contribute to your financial goals.

Balance Sheet

OWN	Balance		OWE	Balance	
Savings Acc	$5,000		Line of Credit	$7,000	
RRSP	$15,000		Credit Card	$0	
TFSA	$50,000				
House	$750,000		Mortgage	$450,000	
Car	$25,000		Car Financing	$15,000	
Total:		$845,000	Total:		$472,000
Net Worth		$373,000			

Anything that is insignificant or is paid off every month, we don't put into our balance sheet as it is only temporary. Things like, maybe our chequing's account balance – if there is no consistent balance in there, we leave off; your credit card – you might use it every month and rack up $3000 a month, but if you consistently pay if off every month, it doesn't go on your balance sheet.

Cash Flow

Remember, we are looking for NET monthly income (after taxes and deductions), not gross. We only care about what actually hits your bank account and leaves your bank account on a monthly basis.

In			Out		
Salary (net)	$4,000		Rent/Mortgage	$3,000	
Salary (spouse)	$4,000		Car payments	$750	
			Car/House Insurance	$350	
			Life/CI/DI	$500	
			Food	$400	
			Entertainment	$500	
			Utilities	$500	
			Misc	$300	
Total:	$8,000		Total:	$6,300	
Monthly Disposable Cash Flow:		$1,700.00			

Your monthly disposable cash flow is the tool you will use to build up your net worth. In the beginning stages, you might have negative net worth, and negative cash flow (especially if you just graduated or are starting fresh). The way to transition to a positive net worth, is working on cleaning up your cash flow. Once your cash flow is positive, then you have money to plan with and to invest. However, you will never become wealthy through only saving, budgeting, and living frugally.

You need to be able to increase your cash flow by increasing your income. If you are a salaried employee, that means getting promotions. If you are running a business, that means growing your business tax efficiently. On top of all of that, you will need to grow other forms of income. All of which will be discussed in the later sections.

"Find your Why."

Financial Planning 2: Goals, Timelines, and Risks

The next step after taking a snap shot and assessing where we are, is to identify our goals. Before we can properly identify our financial goals, we need to understand our life goals. As mentioned before, being wealthy and successful requires us to have achievement and significance.

What are our goals?

- Be successful
- Be wealthy
- Be happy
- Be respected
- ...?

All these terms are relative, as everyone has a different definition for all of the words listed above. Goals are dreams which we action. We put a plan in place to achieve them. Our financial results are a reflection of our personal and career goals.

The easiest way to clarify these goals is to take a look at where you want to be thirty years from now. What is it that you are doing every day? Who's lives have you touched? Who is it you want to be? What impact do you want to make? Pin point what is important to you.

When you get to a point where you feel like its not worth it, questioning yourself and your goals, you need to figure out your why, and if you do - you will be able to push through any obstacle. Figure out your WHY. Your "Why" is the underlying reason you do what you do. They say the best way to pinpoint this, is to ask yourself "why" seven times. The further you drill down, the closer you will get to your primary motivation. Understanding this will give you an internal focus and strength you won't find any where else.

Where I am today, where we (my wife and I) are today – we are very lucky to be. Financially we have achieved more in under five years than most people have or will, working their entire lives. We often ask ourselves how much is enough, and when should we stop. Our net worth today is several million dollars – starting in the negatives several years ago. If we were to "retire" and sell our assets, pay off all of our debt and invest the money – we could easily have a retirement income today of $250,000 - $350,000 a year passively (with a return of 10%-15% annually virtually guaranteed, to be discussed in later sections). This would be a comfortable income for the rest of our lives by any standards.

However, retiring today does not fit into our why. Our why motivates us to keep going, to keep building, because our why is so much bigger than just ourselves. If it was just us, we could happily stop and just live the rest of our lives without much worry. But the why is what drives us to keep on pushing. And until we accomplish that – we will keep going. I hope this book will give you all the tools you need to accomplish your why as well.

Whatever underlying reason you do what you do, who ever that person is you want to be ten, twenty, thirty years from now – you can be that person today. What would the future you do in this situation? How would the future you feel? How would the future you react? Understanding the big picture, makes many things that are happening around you right now, seem trivial. Unless it will negatively impact your big picture, there really is no sense in getting angry or defensive. Focus on the big picture, and let your actions speak. Be the person that you want to become, today.

Once you have a clear picture of who are you – work backwards to fill in the gaps. Figure out the steps along the way to become that person. "Personal" planning is exactly like financial planning. Your career and personal goals will directly impact your financial goals. Developing ourselves, increasing our financial value is the difference between being paid $25/hour or $300/hour. If you are dedicating the majority of your time and energy to someone else's company, make sure they value that. You are sacrificing your personal and financial long term growth. It is an opportunity cost (the gain of you working for your boss needs to be greater than the loss of other opportunities).

How do you put together a personal development plan? Exactly like a financial plan. We start by looking at our Balance Sheet and Cash Flow.

In this case, Cash Flow is now made up of TIME. Your income is composed of Waking Hours. Your expenses are composed of Busy Hours. Your goal is to eliminate as many of those Busy Hours as possible to free up more Disposable Time Flow. This Disposable Time Flow is the tool that you will use to build your Personal Net Worth.

Balance Sheet is now made up of capital (monetary and human). You only have ASSETS (what you own) on the balance sheet and no Liabilities (what you owe). You don't "owe" anyone anything, therefore 0 liabilities. What qualifies as Assets on your Personal Balance Sheet? Skill sets, knowledge, relationships that contribute to generating cash flow and helping you become closer to your future self.

There is a common saying that your network is your networth. Collect mentors, advisors, and consultants to stack up the Asset side of your balance sheet.

When approaching new projects, opportunities and side hustles – remember you don't need to know all the answers. No one expects you to know everything. But your responsibility is knowing where to find these answers and then using these answers to execute your new projects, opportunities and side hustles. Approaching new opportunities is exactly the same as buying a property. You need to save the down payment, and then the bank will provide you the mortgage. You need to make sure you are 10% to 20% ready for the opportunity, and your mentors and advisors will guide you through the other 80% to 90%. And remember to "refinance" when you can! In real estate, refinancing means to borrow equity from your property once it has built up enough. In this case, its about being able to start another project once your current project has built enough credibility for you to do so. Leverage is the key to wealth!

You want to be as focused as possible towards your long term goal. Buffett had a particular method of doing so which I've found to be quite helpful.

Buffett's mentees asked him how he was able to focus his energy and stay on track when there were so many opportunities available. At that point Buffett asked his mentees to create a list of their 25 important things they wanted to do. Then Buffett asked them to narrow the list down the top 5 things they wanted to do. Buffett then asked his mentees, "what do you do with the remaining 20 things you crossed off the list?" One of the mentees said, "that's easy! First, we do the top 5 things, and then with our left over time, we do the other 20 things." To this Buffett replied, "absolutely not, those 20 things are the – stay as far away from as you can things – as they will suck your energy from the 5 most important things you must do."

Take some time now to think about who you want to be, and how you will get there. Create your own list of 25 things, and then narrow it down to 5 non-negotiables things.

Financial planning: Goals

Financial goals follow a certain 1, 2, 3 formula – 1) what you want to use money on, 2) the amount of money needed, 3) when we need the money. The next consideration is what risks do we have? Can we protect against them using insurance? If not, what can we do if we miss our goals? Can we move forward with a lower amount of money and/or can we increase the investment timeline and extend the number of months or years until we reach our goal?

- Financial planning: Goals & Amounts Needed

  - How much money do you need for "enter want"

  - New car, house, child's education, retirement etc.

  - How can we save that much from our cash flows and investment strategies

- Financial planning: Time

  - When do you need that amount of money?

  - Short term (under 2 years), Medium (3-5 years), Long (6+ years)

  - How much risk are you willing to assume?

- Financial planning: Risk

  - What happens if we can't meet your goal

  - Are you willing to decrease your goal and/or extend your timeline

  - Do we have any guarantees in place? Can we build them in?

Goal	Timeline	Possible Risks	Solution
Pay off student loans (20k)	5.5 years	CI/DI	Insurance, extend timeline
New Car (8k)	3 years	CI/DI	Insurance, extend timeline, buy lower end car
Townhouse (80k – down payment and closing costs)	7 years	CI/DI	Insurance, extend timeline, buy lower end property
Retirement (4k/month income)	25 years	CI/DI, LI	Insurance, retire with less monthly income, timeline NON-negotiable

"Your financial future is what you make of it!"

Financial Planning 3: Projections and Recommendations

The last step of our plan is to take our monthly disposable cash flow and apply it to our goals. We want to divide up our disposable cash flow in the correct proportions so that we can meet our goals in our target timelines. How do we know we can meet our goals 5, 10, or even 30 years into the future? We need to make projections to estimate the future value of our money.

The basic projection formulas are below:

1) Future Value = $P (1 + i)^t$
2) Future Value = $d \times \dfrac{(1 + i)^t - 1}{i} \times (1 + i)$

The first formula deals with investing a lump sum of money. For example, if on our balance sheet, we had $15,000 in our TFSA and we were to invest this money for the next 8 years. The variables are as follows:

"P" is the lump sum of $15,000

"t" is the time line either in months or years.

"i" is the annual return of your investment net of inflation. In this example, our timeline "t" is 8 years, which qualifies for a long timeline. Therefore, we can take a higher level of risk. In general, short term timelines between 1-3 years you should take only low risk, and you can expect a bank investment return of 1-3% annually on average. A medium time line is between 4-6 years, and you can expect a bank investment return of 4-6% annually on average. A long timeline of 7 years or longer, you can expect a bank investment return of 7-10% annually on average.

For our purposes, we can estimate inflation as 2% as an average. Therefore, if we expect a bank portfolio return of 8%, then "i" = 8% - 2% = 6%.

The second formula we use with our monthly disposable cash flow. This formula determines the future value of periodic deposits. For our purposes, that means how much money will we have in 8 years, if we continually save $100 per month every month for the next 8 years.

The variables are:

"d" is our monthly or yearly savings amount

"t" is our monthly or yearly time line

"i" is our annual investment return

Let's make an example of the complete financial planning process to tie it all together.

Cash Flow:

In			Out	
Salary (net)	$4,000		Rent/Mortgage	$1,000
			Car payments	$750
			Life/CI/DI	$300
			Food	$400
			Entertainment	$400
			Utilities/Cell Phone/Internet	$200
			Misc	$200
Total:	$4,000		Total:	$3,250
Monthly Disposable Cash Flow:		**$750.00**		

Balance Sheet:

OWN	Balance		OWE	Balance
TFSA	$5,000		Student Loan	$20,000
Car	$25,000		Car Financing	$15,000
Total:	$30,000		Total:	$35,000
Net Worth		-$5,000.00		

Goals:

Goal	Timeline	Possible Risks	Solution
Pay off student loans (20k)	5.5 years	CI/DI	Insurance, extend timeline
Townhouse (80k – down payment and closing costs)	7 years	CI/DI	Insurance, extend timeline, buy lower end property
Retirement (4k/month income)	25 years	CI/DI, LI	Insurance, retire with less monthly income, timeline NON-negotiable

Our next step would be to divide up the $750 monthly disposable income we have, along with the $5,000 we have saved in our TFSAs and apply them to our 3 financial goals using our formulas.

Luckily, I've put together simple plug and play excel spreadsheets when we can simply input numbers to see how our financial goals play out. Find them on www.dumbmoney.ca with videos on how to use the spreadsheets!

Here is how we would use them. The goals are ranked in order of importance, however, we can tackle all these goals at once. The excel sheets projections are broken down into months, so you know how much money you should have by then.

For simplicity sake, we are going to assume that the Student Loans and Down payment on the Townhouse are the same time lines. Technically speaking, we start with $750/month cash flow which we will use $275/month towards the Student Loans, and the remaining $475/month towards the down payment (for a total of $750/month savings). The Student Loan goal we achieve in 5.5 years, while we will continue saving for 1.5 more years for the Townhouse down payment. After 5.5 years, $275/month will return to our monthly disposable cash flows which we can put towards other goals. However, we are going to simplify things and assume the full $750/month is used for the full 7 years.

Here is a snapshot of how that looks like:

Goal 1 (Student Loan):

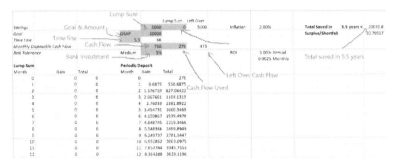

For this goal, we meet our $20,000 goal in the targeted time line of 5.5 years with $30 surplus.

Goal 2 (Town House):

Savings	Goal & Amount	Townhouse	900000	5000	0	Inflation	2.00%	Total Saved in	7 years = $5418.36
Goal								Surplus/Shortfall	-24580.1
Time Line	Time line	7	84						
Monthly Disposable Cash Flow			47%	475	0	ROI	5.00% Annual	Total saved in 7 years	
Risk Tolerance	Remaining Cash Flow	High	7%				0.004167 Monthly	(we are short)	

Lump Sum		Bank investment return	Periodic Deposit		
Month	Gain	Total	Month	Gain	Total
0	0	5000	0		475
1	20.83333	5020.833	1	1.979167	951.97917
2	20.92054	5041.753	2	3.96668	1430.3457
3	21.00731	5062.761	3	5.962274	1911.908
4	21.09454	5083.856	4	7.966283	2394.8743
5	21.18273	5105.038	5	9.978643	2879.8529
6	21.27099	5126.309	6	11.96939	3366.8523
7	21.35962	5147.669	7	14.02855	3855.8809
8	21.44862	5169.118	8	16.09637	4346.3471
9	21.53798	5190.656	9	18.11228	4840.0893
10	21.62773	5212.283	10	20.16691	5335.2267
11	21.71785	5234.001	11	22.23011	5832.4564
12	21.80834	5255.809	12	24.3019	6331.7583

For this goal, after 7 years of saving all of our remaining cash flow of $475/month, we are short $24,580.10. Therefore, at this point we have two options – either buy a smaller, cheaper home, and/or continue saving for a longer period of time, and/or take a higher risk investment in hopes of getting a higher return.

After 7 years, our full cash flow returns to us, $750/month is what we can now use for our retirement planning. In retirement the key, is outliving your money. This requires two calculations – how much money will you have at your targeted retirement age or date. How long until you run out of money. In this example we targeted a

$4,000/month lifestyle in retirement. One of the mistakes a lot of people make is forgetting to include inflation during their retirement. We (hopefully) will retire for a great number of years 25, 35, 45, or even 55 years or longer in some cases. Therefore what $4,000 will purchase a lot more for you in your first year of retirement compared to your 40th year of retirement. To combat this, every month we need to withdraw slightly more money.

Here is how that looks –

Goal 3 Retirement: (note our timeline is 18 years which is 25 years minus the 7 years we spent saving to repay Goal 1, and buy Goal 2)

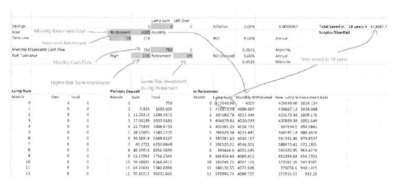

In 18 years, we have only grown our money to a total of $413,650. This is nearly not enough to retire on, especially if we want to be able to maintain a $4,000 per month lifestyle. (Note: that every month after month 1 of retirement, we withdraw slightly more than $4,000 to offset the 2% yearly inflation assumption we made). If we retire at 60, we can expect to live until 85 or 90 years old at a least, therefore we will need enough money to live at least 25 to 30 years.

From the snap shot below, we determine that we run out of money in month 108, which is only 9 years of retirement. That means that if we retired at age 55, we need run out of money at age 64.

92	0	0	92	741.4418	100350.35		92	74522.248	4662.259	69859.989	174.65
93	0	0	93	752.6276	101852.97		93	70034.639	4670.029	65364.61	163.4115
94	0	0	94	763.8973	103366.87		94	65528.021	4677.813	60850.209	152.1255
95	0	0	95	775.2515	104892.12		95	61002.334	4685.609	56316.725	140.7918
96	0	0	96	786.6909	106428.81		96	56457.517	4693.418	51764.099	129.4102
97	0	0	97	798.2161	107977.03		97	51893.509	4701.241	47192.268	117.9807
98	0	0	98	809.8277	109536.86		98	47310.249	4709.076	42601.173	106.5029
99	0	0	99	821.5264	111108.18	At this	99	42707.676	4716.925	37990.751	94.97688
100	0	0	100	833.3129	112691.7	point, we	100	38085.728	4724.786	33360.942	83.40235
101	0	0	101	845.1877	114286.88	run out of	101	33444.344	4732.661	28711.683	71.77921
102	0	0	102	857.1516	115894.04	money	102	28783.463	4740.549	24042.914	60.10729
103	0	0	103	869.2053	117513.24		103	24103.021	4748.449	19354.572	48.38643
104	0	0	104	881.3493	119144.59		104	19402.958	4756.364	14646.595	36.61649
105	0	0	105	893.5844	120788.18		105	14683.211	4764.291	9918.9205	24.7973
106	0	0	106	905.9113	122444.09		106	9943.7178	4772.231	5171.4865	12.92872
107	0	0	107	918.3306	124112.42		107	5184.4152	4780.185	404.23022	1.010576
108	0	0	108	930.8431	125793.26		108	405.24379	4788.152	-4382.9112	-10.9573
109	0	0	109	943.4495	127486.71		109	-4393.8858	4796.132	-9190.0007	-22.975
110	0	0	110	956.1503	129192.86		110	-9212.9757	4804.126	-14017.101	-35.0428
111	0	0	111	968.9465	130911.81		111	-14052.144	4812.133	-18864.277	-47.1607

At this point we have determined that we miss goal 2, and goal 3.

Now we need to analyze what can we do, to make our financial plan more efficient. Now remember, in the RRSP section, I mentioned the only way I would ever use the RRSP account is for the First Time Home Buyers Plan.

Take a minute to re-read that section.

Now let's put that knowledge to work.

According to our Goal 2 Excel sheet, in 7 years we have saved a total of $55,420. Firstly, if our risk tolerance allows it – we will want to take a bit more risk for potentially a bit higher gain. So, we will move our expected average return from 7% to 10%. This will take the total amount we've saved during the 7 years from $55,420 to $62,820.

See below:

Savings			5000	Lump Sum 5000	Left Over 0	Inflation	2.00%		Total Saved in	7 years =	62820.36
Goal		Townhouse	80000						Surplus/Shortfall		-17179
Time Line		7		84							
Monthly Disposable Cash Flow			475	475	0						
Risk Tolerance		High	10%			ROI	8.00% Annual				
							0.006667 Monthly				

Lump Sum			Periodic Deposit								
Month	Gain	Total	Month	Gain	Total						
0	0	5000	0		475						
1	33.33333	5033.333	1	3.166667	953.16667						
2	33.55556	5066.889	2	6.354444	1434.5211						
3	33.77926	5100.668	3	9.563474	1919.0846						
4	34.00445	5134.673	4	12.7939	2406.8785						
5	34.23115	5168.904	5	16.04586	2897.9243						
6	34.45936	5203.363	6	19.3195	3392.2438						
7	34.68909	5238.052	7	22.61496	3889.8588						
8	34.92035	5272.973	8	25.93239	4390.7912						
9	35.15315	5308.126	9	29.27194	4805.0631						
10	35.3875	5343.513	10	32.63375	5402.6960						
11	35.62342	5379.137	11	36.01798	5913.7149						
12	35.86091	5414.998	12	39.42477	6428.1396						

If you've been reading, you have been investing your funds inside of your TFSA account. In February of year 7, you know that using the First Time Home Buyers Plan, we take $35,000 from our TFSA account and dump it all into our RRSP account (of which we will borrow the $35,000 from when the time comes to buy our property). By May or June of year 7, we will get a very large tax rebate. If we are netting $4,000 per month from our job, that means our annual salary is around $60,000. Although our marginal tax rate is around 30%, the average tax return we can expect will be less since we are making such a large contribution. (I like to use the Ernest & Young RRSP Rebate Calculator – just Google E & Y Tax Calculator and you will find it). Therefore, we can expect a cheque from the government of about $8,358.

With this tax rebate, it takes our total amount saved from $62,820, to $71,178 in a matter of months ($35,000 in RRSPs, $27,820 in TFSAs, and $8,358 in our chequings account from the tax rebate). We are still a bit short of our $80,000 goal, however, we are much closer than before.

Originally, we were $24,580 short, and now, we are only $8,822 short which is a huge difference with just a few tweaks to our financial plan. A $8,822 savings deficit can easily be overcome with some smart negotiating on our purchase price (winning negotiations will be discussed in the later sections).

Note: CMHC now has a new program where they will match up your down payment up to a total of 10% of the purchase price of the property. However, they will own that portion of your property until you sell, at which time whatever percentage of the property they own will be repaid to them. Ie. If you bought your house for $500,000 and CMHC lent you $50,000 for that purchase, they own 10%. In 10 years time, when you sell that house for $1,000,000, CMHC receives 10% which is $100,000 as a repayment. Would I use this loan/home ownership partnership? Probably not – if you can get there by yourself, the rewards financially will be so much greater. However, if this is your ONLY way to get into the real estate market, then go for it.

Next, let's tackle retirement.

Let's take a bit more risk and change our expected bank returns from 11% to 13% during our working life. During retirement, we want to leave our risk tolerance the same since we will be using this money every month, we don't want to take a large investment loss. So we will leave our expected bank returns at 5%. Next, rather than retire 25 years from today, let's push out our timeline to 30 years. This takes our savings timeline from 18 years to 23 years. See below for the results.

		Lump Sum	Left Over						
Savings		0	0	0	Inflation	2.00%	0.0016667	Total Saved in 23 years =	942824.2
Goal		Retirement	4000 monthly					Surplus/Shortfall	
Time Line		23	276		ROI	11.00%	Annual		
Monthly Disposable Cash Flow		750	750	0			0.009167	Monthly	
Risk Tolerance		High	13% Retirement 5%		ROI (retired)	4.00%	Annual		
							0.003333	Monthly	

Lump Sum			Periodic Deposit			In Retirement				
Month	Gain	Total	Month	Gain	Total	Month	Lump Sum	Monthly Withdrawal	New Lump Sum	Reinvestment Gain
0	0	0	0		750	0	942824.21	4000	938824.21	3129.414
1	0	0	1	6.875	1506.875	1	941953.62	4006.667	937946.96	3126.49
2	0	0	2	13.81902	2270.688	2	941073.45	4013.344	937060.1	3123.534
3	0	0	3	20.81464	3041.5027	3	940183.64	4020.033	936163.6	3120.545
4	0	0	4	27.88044	3819.3831	4	939284.15	4026.733	935257.42	3117.525
5	0	0	5	35.01101	4604.3941	5	938374.94	4033.445	934341.5	3114.472
6	0	0	6	42.20695	5396.6011	6	937455.97	4040.167	933415.8	3111.386
7	0	0	7	49.46884	6196.0699	7	936527.19	4046.901	932480.29	3108.268
8	0	0	8	56.79731	7002.8672	8	935588.55	4053.645	931534.91	3105.116
9	0	0	9	64.19299	7817.0602	9	934640.02	4060.402	930570.62	3101.932
10	0	0	10	71.65638	8638.7165	10	933681.55	4067.169	929614.39	3098.715
11	0	0	11	79.18823	9467.9048	11	932713.1	4073.948	928639.15	3095.464
12	0	0	12	86.78913	10304.694	12	931734.62	4080.737	927653.88	3092.18

By increasing our risk slightly and adding 5 more working years, we've managed to increase our retirement savings from $413,650 to a massive $942,824. That is MORE than double our original retirement amount.

In retirement, we are able to take our retirement from 108 months to a lengthy 262 months! That is almost 22 years of retirement compared to a measly 9 years in the original plan. Although we've managed to do better than before at a retirement age of 60, we run out of money at age 82. Another thing to note is, to achieve an average return of anything over 10% with a bank fund is highly unlikely.

251	0	0	251	6658.81	733824.4	251	67943.808	6075.592	61868.216	154.6705
252	0	0	252	6726.724	741301.13	252	62022.886	6085.718	55937.168	139.8429
253	0	0	253	6795.26	748846.39	253	56077.011	6095.861	49981.15	124.9529
254	0	0	254	6864.425	756460.81	254	50106.103	6106.021	44000.082	110.0002
255	0	0	255	6934.224	764145.04	255	44110.082	6116.198	37993.885	94.98471
256	0	0	256	7004.663	771899.7	256	38088.869	6126.391	31962.478	79.9062
257	0	0	257	7075.747	779725.45	257	32042.384	6136.602	25905.782	64.76446
258	0	0	258	7147.483	787622.93	258	25970.547	6146.83	19823.717	49.55929
259	0	0	259	7219.877	795592.81	259	19873.277	6157.074	13716.202	34.29051
260	0	0	260	7292.934	803635.74	260	13750.493	6167.336	7583.1569	18.95789
261	0	0	261	7366.661	811752.4	261	7602.1148	6177.615	1424.4999	3.56125
262	0	0	262	7441.064	819943.47	262	1428.0612	6187.911	-4759.8498	-11.8996
263	0	0	263	7516.148	828209.61	263	-4771.7494	6198.224	-10969.974	-27.4249
264	0	0	264	7591.921	836551.54	264	-10997.399	6208.555	-17205.953	-43.0149
265	0	0	265	7668.389	844969.92	265	-17248.968	6218.902	-23467.87	-58.6697

Not to worry, because in the later sections we will discuss where to invest and how to invest with minimal risk, and a much higher return than compared to our regular bank investments. Your financial future is what you make it!

"Your worst case scenario will be better than most people's best case scenario."

Section 5: Financial Planning for Entrepreneurs

Being an entrepreneur, whether its your main hustle or a side hustle, you have a distinct advantage over the regular employee on your path to becoming wealthy. Somewhere, within all of us is an entrepreneur.

The Canadian tax system has particular tax advantages for small business corporations. In this section, we will run through the basics to advanced loop holes for us to exponentially and explosively grow our networth.

Business owners are vulnerable to the regular threats to any financial plan – longevity, volatility, income, inflation and taxes in life and in death.

However, business owners unlike the regular employee have an amazing tool at their disposal. The ability to incorporate their main hustle or side hustle(s). Incorporating your business has several advantages: i) limited liability, ii) tax incentives, iii) tax deferral, iv) income splitting, v) advanced insurance strategies

Once you incorporate your business, your business becomes a separate legal and tax entity. This protects your business from any personal threats, and protects your personal assets from any business threats. This means, if anyone sues your business, your personal assets are protected – only your business assets are at risk. This grants you limited liability.

This also means, that your business will outlive you if you wish. If your corporation is structured properly, it can continue to operate and produce an income for your loved ones for generations to come. This is such a powerful tool in terms of financial planning.

Corporations (in Ontario) enjoy approximately a 15% active business income tax (on the first $500,000 of taxable income). (Note: Different provinces have a different total active business income tax rates which vary by a few percentage points, but are all lower than the average personal tax rate.) This is a big difference between the personal income tax rate which can range on average from 20% to 52%. Active business income is defined as income generated from the operations of the business. This means, if you run an interior decorating company, active business income is the income your business made from decorating homes. Passive income is income generated from investments. Corporations can invest just like individuals can.

When you withdraw funds from your corporation you need to pay yourself either as salary and/or dividend. This subjects you to the personal income tax rates regular employees face for the amount that you pay yourself. Dividend tax rates can be at high at 39%. Therefore, to avoid these taxes, we want to leave as much money in the corporation as possible. We only want to withdraw enough money to pay for our personal monthly expenses, anything extra, we want to leave in the corporation to limit our taxes paid at 15%. It is more beneficial to us to invest the funds within the corporate shelter, rather than take it out, get taxed as personal income, and then invest with the after tax dollars.

To show you the power of incorporating, the below simplified example is the difference between being a sole proprietor and or salaried employee compared to an incorporated business owner.

	Incorporated	Not Incorporated
Gross Income	$380,000	$380,000
Expenses	($100,000)	($100,000)
After Expenses	$280,000	$280,000
Taxes	($42,000)	($113,693)
Net After Taxes	$238,000 (Held in Corp)	$166,307 (In personal bank acc)
Salary	$138,000	-
Taxes	($41,699)	-
Net Personal Income	$96,301	-
Left in the Corp	$100,000	-
Total Income	$196,301	$166,307

The above table shows two difference scenarios for the same person; i) an incorporated business owner, ii) a non-incorporated business owner (also known as a sole proprietor).

In our example, we want to keep as much as we can consistent. The first line is Gross Income (before expenses and taxes), which is $380,000 annually for both. The second line are the Expenses for running the business, which is $100,000 for both (it is in red and in brackets, as it is a cost). The third line shows that after we pay our expenses, we have $280,000 left in our bank account. At the end of the year, we need to pay our taxes. This is where the 1st difference happens. The Corporation enjoys a 15% income tax resulting in $42,000 in taxes paid whereas, the sole proprietor is taxed personally resulting in $133,696 taxes paid. The fifth line shows the amount left over – the corporation has $238,000 while the sole proprietor has only $166,307. This is the end of the story for the sole proprietor.

However, for the incorporated business owner, we still haven't paid ourselves yet. We worked hard the entire year so we want to enjoy ourselves. The incorporated business owner pays themselves $138,000 as a salary (normally you would want to divide the total amount into salary and dividend, and possibly split the amount between family members to reduce taxes). The personal taxes on $138,000 result in $41,699 in taxes paid, netting a personal income of $96,301 in the personal bank account. In the corporate bank account, there is $100,000 left over (after paying corporate taxes, the corporate account had $238,000, which we then paid ourselves $138,000 as a salary, leaving $100,000). Therefore in total, the corporation generated for us $196,301 net of taxes ($96,301 net personal income and $100,000 net corporate income).

This means, we generated an extra $30,000 per year, just by incorporating and understanding the basic usage of the corporate structure. Imagine what you can do with an extra $30,000 every single year. Imagine if you re-invested this money to grow the business (hiring another employee, buying new machinery, developing new tech) or even just investing this money for your retirement. Just a small tweak in how you manage your finances can have a relatively large result which accumulates and snow balls year after year.

In the example below, your corporation makes $116k per year taxable income (after all expenses have been paid). After taxes you will have 100k left over in the corporation (as per the example above as well). This money will sit inside your corporate bank unless you decide to withdraw it.

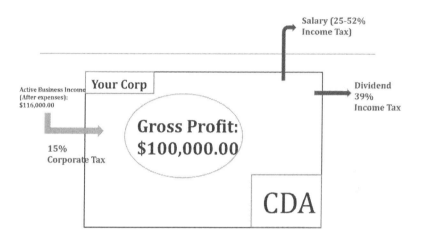

So now every year, there is $100,000 gathering in the corporate bank account. Year after year, this money is building up, but to remove it from the corporation, there will be huge tax implications as you can see from the red arrows. This is the dilemma business owners face – keep the money trapped in the corporation or withdraw it, and be subjected to a huge tax bill.

This is a problem which the majority of business owners face. Luckily for you, I'm about to teach you a strategy to access and extract the funds tax free.

In the diagram above, built into your corporation is a specialized account, called the Capital Dividends Account (CDA). For our purposes, we will call it the Tax Free Zone. Any money that goes into this account, can come out tax free bypassing the Salary and Dividend income tax. You can think of this account as your corporation's TFSA. However, this isn't a physical account that you can walk into your bank and open. It is an imaginary account which your accountant needs to keep track of.

Because this account is so powerful, there are limits to what can go into this account. The government is not about to let business owners dump all of their money into the Tax Free Zone and bypass all the personal taxes. It is up to you to strategically plan and build this account up.

There are two main ways for a business owner to build up their Tax Free Zone. Firstly, through Capital Gains. As we spoke about in the investment section, only 50% of the capital gains is taxable, and the other 50% is non-taxable. Corporations are able to enjoy this as well. So, 50% of the corporation's capital gains are non-taxable, and these amount flows into the Tax Free Zone and is able to pass to the business owner tax free. The corporation can purchase mutual funds, ETFs, stocks, buy real estate etc to build up short term capital gains to offset the business owner's taxable income needs. (The other taxable 50% of capital gains is taxed at 50%).

The second way, which is more of a long term strategy, is to use Universal or Participating whole life insurance. I prefer to use Participating Whole Life primarily because business is cyclical. This means that if the market is down, your business will likely be slowing down as well. Even though your business is slowing down and revenue is lower than usual, you still need to pay your fixed operating expenses. These things might include office rent/mortgage, office utilities, employee salaries etc. When this happens, you will need to draw on your investments to keep the business afloat. The worst thing that could happen, is that your investments are down inside of your corporation investment account as well as your Universal policy, and you are withdrawing from them as now they won't have time to recover with the market.

Participating Whole Life as we have already discussed does not move with the market, therefore will act as a safe haven for your money. I use Par as exactly that, a safe haven. The PAR is my worst case scenario. Even if everything goes wrong, as long as I am able to maintain my PAR premiums, than that will be the minimum amount of money I will have to leverage for my retirement. Everything on top on the PAR (all of my other investments and projects), is a bonus. Therefore, it is beneficial to understand your minimum must haves financially to be happy, guarantee that you will be able to get it, and then you won't need to worry about your financial future ever. This will allow you to grasp relatively risky opportunities easier since you aren't worried about possible losses, because you have already allotted enough funds into your "worst" case scenario. If you do this properly, your worst case scenario will be better than most people's best case scenario.

For a 30 year old male, non-smoking, average health - the policy illustration is shown below:

Policy Year Deposits (EOY)	Total Deposits *	Total Insurance Premium *	Annual Dividend **	Enhanced Coverage Term Additions ***	Paid-Up Additions	Total Coverage Amount	Total Paid-Up Values	Total Cash Surrender Values
1	$12,000	$12,000	$1,562	$458,404	$0	$882,853	$16,439	$4,334
2	$12,000	$12,000	$3,137	$449,807	$8,597	$882,853	$44,370	$10,897
3	$12,000	$12,000	$3,286	$432,586	$25,818	$882,853	$83,665	$18,461
4	$12,000	$12,000	$3,457	$415,203	$43,201	$882,853	$125,757	$27,108
5	$12,000	$12,000	$3,650	$397,563	$60,841	$882,853	$170,599	$36,913
6	$12,000	$12,000	$3,857	$379,565	$78,839	$882,853	$210,201	$46,347
7	$12,000	$12,000	$4,058	$361,180	$97,224	$882,853	$250,136	$56,479
8	$12,000	$12,000	$4,289	$342,470	$115,934	$882,853	$290,319	$67,350
9	$12,000	$12,000	$4,500	$323,447	$134,957	$882,853	$330,731	$79,001
10	$12,000	$12,000	$4,750	$304,076	$154,328	$882,853	$371,359	$91,473
15	$12,000	$12,000	$6,349	$200,877	$257,527	$882,853	$579,284	$167,894
20	$12,000	$12,000	$8,559	$83,256	$375,148	$882,853	$799,597	$273,345
25	$0	$0	$7,785	$0	$475,291	$899,740	$899,740	$359,655
30	$0	$0	$10,468	$0	$580,385	$1,004,814	$1,004,814	$471,165
35	$0	$0	$14,211	$0	$701,620	$1,126,269	$1,126,269	$613,431
40	$0	$0	$19,434	$0	$845,171	$1,269,620	$1,269,620	$792,277
45	$0	$0	$26,550	$0	$1,017,844	$1,442,293	$1,442,293	$1,013,166
50	$0	$0	$35,775	$0	$1,228,493	$1,652,942	$1,652,942	$1,281,267
55	$0	$0	$47,054	$0	$1,485,917	$1,910,366	$1,910,366	$1,601,863
60	$0	$0	$59,978	$0	$1,797,753	$2,222,202	$2,222,202	$1,981,272
65	$0	$0	$72,882	$0	$2,167,479	$2,591,928	$2,591,928	$2,431,874
70	$0	$0	$67,637	$0	$2,567,282	$2,991,731	$2,991,731	$3,059,368

The first column is "Policy Year," which is the number of years which you've had the policy. For most PAR policies, you have the option of paying the policy all in 1 year, 8 years, or 20 years. For this illustration, we've chosen investing in the PAR for 20 years. Therefore, after 20 years you don't need to invest into the policy anymore but it will continue to grow, you can see that the column showing $0 under "Total Deposits" after year 20 onwards.

The 2nd columns shows the yearly total deposit amount $12,000 a year, which is $1,000 per month.

The 3rd most left column "Total Coverage Amount" is your death benefit. When you die, this amount will pass into your Tax Free Zone, and be available to your shareholders TAX FREE, right away. (Therefore, it is important to make your loved ones non-voting shareholders so they may access the money in the corporation).

However, what we care most about is – what happens while we are alive? How can we build up our money tax efficiently? How can we make sure our money is protected from taxes in death as well? This last question we answered just above. So now lets make sure we keep as much of our money as possible. That is the last column "Total Cash Surrender Value." This is the CSV we have been talking about. This amount is your bank account. Every year this money grows tax free. How we want to use this money ideally, is to maximize the value of the money. This means, we want 100% of the money to continue growing – to maximize the year over year tax free growth, while having money to use today for whatever we wish. Remember previously, we said the best way to use the money is to leverage it out.

To do this, we would take our policy annual statement (every year the insurance company will send you a letter showing you how much money you have in your CSV) to the bank (to the head office, branch level employees will have no idea what you are talking about) and get a secured line of credit for 90% loan to value of the CSV. From the illustration, we see that in 35 years, when we are 65 we have $613,431 – meaning we will have a LOC of $552,087 (90% of $613,431) to use. Normally, you would use this to cover your living expenses to minimize any withdrawals from taxable income sources (RRSPs, Group pensions, CPP etc).

For example, if we use $4,000 per month from the LOC it would take about 10 years for you to use the money. 10 years later, your CSV has grown from $613,431 to $1,013,166 at which point you would re-leverage 90% of the new amount which is $911,849, giving us another $359,762.40 to use. At this point, we are now 75 years old we can draw $3000 per month from our LOC, and draw a bit more of our taxable income (RRSP, Group Pensions, CPP – note, at age 71, your have to begin drawing down on your RRSP as it converts into a RIF, retirement income fund), combined with our TFSAs. 10 years later, our CSV has grown to $1,601,863 and we will receive 90% of this again which is $1,441,676.70, meaning we have another $529,837.70 to use ($1,441,676 - $911,849). 10 years later, the CSV grows to $2,431,874, resulting in a LOC of 2,188,686 freeing up an additional $747,010 for us to use for the next 10 years. At this point we are 95 years old – if we were to die at age 100 (policy year 70 in the 1st column), our death benefit would be $2,991,731 which would first pay off the LOC we have used ($2,188,686) resulting in $803,045 passing over tax free to our loved ones (who are non-voting shareholders of the corporation).

As you can see, by investing $1000 per month for 20 years (a total of $240,000), we are able to guarantee a very comfortable retirement with no risk of running out of money. We have successfully built a money tree!

Note: PAR policies grow faster for women versus men keeping all the other variables equal. So, you can imagine that my wife's PAR policy has a higher investment amount than mine to maximize the efficiency of the growth of both policies together.

Note: The above strategy can be used by non-business owners as well.

Now, we will take a look at how effective PAR policies are in combination with regular investments, compared to only regular investments in the following two scenarios:

Scenario 1: Investments only

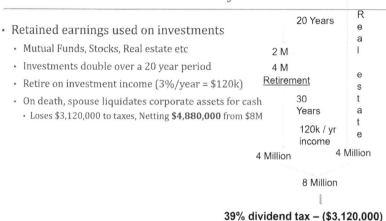

- Retained earnings used on investments
  - Mutual Funds, Stocks, Real estate etc
  - Investments double over a 20 year period
  - Retire on investment income (3%/year = $120k)
  - On death, spouse liquidates corporate assets for cash
    - Loses $3,120,000 to taxes, Netting **$4,880,000** from $8M

$100,000 / year

20 Years

R
e
a
l

e
s
t
a
t
e

2 M

4 M

Retirement

30
Years

120k / yr
income

4 Million   4 Million

8 Million

39% dividend tax – ($3,120,000)

In our original example, the corporation every year has a left over $100,000. In Scenario 1, we are investing the $100,000 in a regular bank investment in our corporate investment account. We run the business for 20 years, which means over a 20 year period, we have accumulated $2,000,000 in our corporate account – with minimal growth we can say the money grew to $4,000,000. (Normally, you can expect your money to double every 10 years as long as you receive an average of 7% annual return.) The corporation also owns the business real estate space.

After 20 years, we decide to retire. Our investment portfolio is now $4,000,000. Let's say our goal is to live off of the investment returns, to preserve the capital (which is the $4,000,000). If we invest in a conservative portfolio we can expect a return of only 3% annually, which means we will receive investment income of $120,000 per year for our retirement. This will last until we die as we only use $120,000 per year, thus protecting the full $4,000,000. We die in 30 years. At this point, for our loved ones to access the money in the corporation, they need to withdraw the money as dividends (which is the most tax efficient at this point). If on death, we had $4,000,000 in investments, and $4,000,000 in real estate

119

than in total our corporation has $8,000,000 in assets. If our family wants to access all the money right away, they would need to pay $3,120,000 in dividend taxes, meaning rather than leaving behind $8,000,000 to our family, we have only left behind $4,880,000.

Scenario 2: Investments & Life Insurance

$50,000 / Year		$50,000 / Year

- Divide retain earnings
  - 50% to investments, 50% to Life Insurance (Par)
  - In retirement, 3% income from investments &
  - Borrow from life insurance (60k/year)
  - Resulting in the same $120k/year income
  - On death – spouse/family net **$11.66M**

```
                              $50,000 / Year          $50,000 / Year

                              20 Years      R            IRP
                                            e
                                            a
        In retirement...      1 M           l            2 M
                              2 M
                                            e
        Retirement            s          Retirement
                              30 Years     t
                                           a          30
                              60k / yr     t          Years
                              income       e          60k / yr
                                                      income      6 M
                  2 Million        4 Million    8 Million
                                                                  2 M
                              6 Million                     8 Million
                                  |                        CDA
        39% dividend tax – ($2,340,000)                    Credit
```

In this second scenario, we are splitting the $100,000 into two buckets – regular investments, and a PAR policy $50,000 per year in each. (This strategy is sometimes called the IRP – which stands for Insured Retirement Plan). After 20 years, we have invested a total of $1,000,000 which conservatively double to $2,000,000 in our bank investment mutual fund. Our PAR policy's CSV is also at $2,000,000 after 20 years. We retire at the 20 year mark, our investments gain 3% per year which gives us $60,000 in investment income, and we withdraw $60,000 per year from our PAR's CSV. Therefore, for the next 30 years, we receive the same total yearly income of $120,000. After 30 years of retirement, we die. At this point, the "magic" of the IRP strategy happens.

Our investment portfolio is $2,000,000 and our real estate is still $4,000,000. When we die, and our family wants withdraw the $6,000,000, there will be a 39% dividend tax which means $2,340,000 will be lost to taxes, leaving only $3,660,000 to our family. The good news is, the PAR pays out $8,000,000 tax free. (The LOC repayment has already been considered since we have only used minimal gains of 3% on the CSV, our principal is protected). Therefore, our family now has $3,600,000 (from the investment plus real estate after taxes) AND $8,000,000 for a total of $11,660,000! That is a HUGE difference compared to scenario 1, in which our family is only left with $4,880,000. That's a difference of an additional $6,780,000 just by changing where we allocate our money! Small tweaks to your financial plan, how you execute, and where you put your money will make a massive change in your life, and your family's life.

Now remember, if we are incorporated, this strategy of using PAR is much cheaper than if we do it personally since if we are paying for the PAR using corporate after tax money at a 15% tax rate, compared to personal after tax money at a 25-52% tax rate. See numeric example below:

	Corporately Owned	Personally Owned
Gross Revenue/Salary Needed	$59,000	$104,000
Taxes Paid (15% vs 52%)	($9,000)	($54,000)
Net available for Par Premiums	$50,000	$50,000

As you can see, personally you will need to make $104,000 to purchase the same $50,000 per year PAR, whereas if you were incorporated, your business would only need to make $59,000 for the same $50,000 PAR.

Now remember, even as an incorporated business owner, you still want to protect and bullet proof your financial plan. To lower your income taxes, and more importantly, to get the government to pay for your protection – make a RRSP contribution so the rebate is large enough to pay for your DI policy with ROP. Calculate the ROP you will receive on your DI policy, and use that money to fund for CI policy with ROP. When you no longer need your CI policy, cash it in for the ROP and use that tax free money to fund part of your retirement!

See numeric example below:

Protecting the Plan: Insurance (owned Personally)

- Assuming you take a salary of $100,000/year,
- Maximum RRSP contributions
  - $18,000 contributions = $7,500/year Tax rebate to fund Disability protection
  - Disability Return of premium to fund Critical Illness protection
  - Critical Illness Return of premium to fund retirement

  - The result? **"Free" protection!**

Protecting the Plan: Insurance (owned Personally)

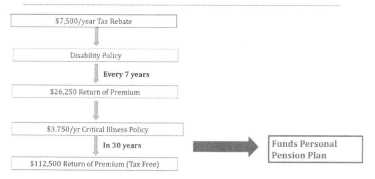

(Note: the healthier you are, and the younger you are – the cheaper the insurance premiums, the faster your CSV builds up. A lot of parents and grandparents buy PAR on their kids and grandkids and transfer ownership of the policy to the child when they turn a certain age (usually 18 years old or later). It is a great way to pass on wealth in a tax efficient manner.)

Note: Participating Whole Life seems like magic but remember it needs a good 15 years to build up a sizable amount in the CSV, so remember to balance your short term income needs with short term investments with the longer term PAR tax efficient strategy.

"The problem is, you don't know what you don't know."

Section 6: Alternative Investments

Here we GOOOOOOOOO!

Now that you know what main stream investments are, and where they will get you (no where fast) – let's get you to where you want to go FAST (fast, not instantly – every plan takes time and proper execution). The problem is, you don't know what you don't know.

Private Mortgages

This is how my mom was able to afford to retire. Like most Canadian immigrants, she was taught to hate debt and value home ownership. She absolutely loves her house, and a major life goal was to be mortgage free – which she achieved around the age of 60. That's great, except you can't eat bricks, or cash them in to pay for your living expenses and property tax. My mom had put all of her savings into her house with a market value of well over $1M, which meant, she had nothing to live on for retirement. So here was the situation, my mom had a house worth well over $1,000,000 and very little relatively in terms of retirement savings. Property taxes alone on the house were close to $8,000 per year, which is close to $700 per month, which pretty much offsets her CPP benefits from the government. So now, how was she supposed to feed herself, pay for utilities, and entertainment very month as was promised in the ideal retirement lifestyle we are sold by the media?

My mom has been retired for several years now, and when she began her retirement, I was in no position financially to support a six figure lifestyle which is the least she deserved for all the sacrifices and hard work through out her life. (Remember, just over 4 years ago, I had just completed my MBA, and racked up almost six figures in student debt).

How did I manage to give my mom the retirement she deserved? Through private mortgages. Using my income, I re-financed my mom's house for her, and used the bank money (cheap debt) to lend. This netted my mom an average of a 12% return annually using the bank's money. Use other people's money (particularly the bank's) to make more money.

From then on, my mom travels 4-6 times a year around the world with trips spanning up to 6 weeks at a time. She loves cruises and her house, and now, she has both and so much more.

What are private mortgages? These are basically GICs that pay 12-18% a year.

This is the world of private mortgages. How would you like to be the bank? How would you like to make money the same way the bank does – through interest and fees, safely and securely? Welcome to the world of private mortgages!

As bank mortgages get harder to qualify for, that provides opportunities for people like us, to fill the gap and lend to those that the banks won't. There are plenty of good people out there that are looking for money but the banks won't give it to them.

These are people such as business owners (who don't show a lot of income to avoid taxes), new immigrants (who have a lot of cash, but no credit history or enough income), or people with good cash flow but poor credit score. As private lenders, we don't really worry about these things. The only thing we care about is how much equity is in the property – the amount of equity in the property is our safety net. We don't take risk if we don't need to. Let me explain.

We use the same criteria the bank uses – we don't lend over 80% LTV. Here is how it works:

We as the investor, we lend our money to the borrower. We do so, for interest income, which is usually in the range of 12-15%. On top of the interest cost, there are Lender Fees (this belongs to you, as you are the lender), and Broker Fees (this belongs to the individual who brokered/or managed the deal). Lender fees and broker fees are usually 2-2.5% each.

For example, a client has a property appraised at $1,500,000 (note: always get an appraisal on a property to get a proper assessment of the fair market value). They currently have an existing bank mortgage of $650,000. This mortgage is in first position, meaning that your loan is in second position. This matters because when the property is sold, the bank will be paid back first (first position), and then you will (second position), and the remaining amount will go to the owner of the property (the amount of equity in the property).

On this 1.5M property, the client is looking to borrow an additional $300,000 for "insert reason." The maximum LTV you should ever lend is 80%, meaning the maximum total loan on the property should not exceed $1,200,000 (80% LTV of $1,500,000). Therefore an additional $300,000 is within the 80% LTV – so the loan makes sense. Normally, I won't go over 75% however there are some instances where I will make an exception. The LTV is up to you, I wouldn't recommend anything above 80%. Also, never lend longer than 1 year at a time.

How to you make sure you get your interest payments, your fees and more importantly protect your capital? Firstly, for the capital amount that you loan, your lawyer will put a LIEN on the client's property. The ensures that if the property is sold, you get the amount of money you originally lent ($300,000). Secondly, protecting your interest and fee income, you take the full yearly amount off the top. This means that if the interest is 12%, your lender fee is 2.5%, and the broker fee is 2.5% (you can also be the broker – to do so, you needed to have obtained the client and then arrange with your lawyer to prepare all the paperwork. If you need a template of the paperwork, feel free to reach out), then the total cost of the loan for the client is 17%. Let's pretend that you are the lender, and the broker. In our example, you are lending $300,000, therefore, you will receive $51,000 (17% of $300,000) when the deal closes and the client will receive the balance of $249,000. $51,000 in one deal is not a bad day's work – and at minimal risk as well!

Taking the interest upfront instead of monthly does two things – firstly, the client doesn't need to worry about paying you monthly for an entire year allowing the client to work on their cash flow and credit score. Secondly, you don't need to worry about chasing the client down for bounced cheques.

What happens after in 1 year? The client can either renew with you for another year, in which case, they will need to pay the interest up front, and pay a renewal fee (usually 1 – 1.5%). Renewals are generally cheaper since there is no broker involved. If you choose not to allow the client to renew and you would like your $300,000 back, the client will need to repay you the full amount at the 1 year anniversary mark (normally the client does this by re-financing the total loan amount at the bank, or they find a new private lender to give them a new 2nd mortgage to replace yours). If they cannot pay (which means they default), you have the right to sell their property. Built into the contract are the consequences of defaulting – whether this is on their monthly payments or the principal amount.

If you are forced to sell their property, this legal process is known as a Power of Sale. This is why we always take the precaution of never going above 75 or 80% LTV. If we need to sell the property at a lower price for a quick sale, then that equity buffer will protect our investment. In this example, if the market price of the property is $1,500,000; we might put it up for sale for $1,350,000 to sell it as quickly as possible. Because the total lending on this property is only $950,000 ($650,000 to the bank, and $300,000 to us), our investment is protected. If we had lent all the way up to $1,400,000 and sold the property for $1,350,000 – we would risk losing $50,000.

In general, as long as you are lending on properties in prime areas (areas with high demand), there is very little risk of a property value decrease.

NOTE: The client always pays the legal fees for themselves and the lender. This can be taken off the top, or the client can pay it in cash – whichever is easier. Usually all the top is easiest.

Rental Properties

Rental properties are great. I personally love real estate. Real estate is the only time the banks will give you such large leverage at such low interest rates. If you are putting only 5% down, then the bank is lending you 95%. (If you declare the property as your primary residence, then you can qualify for the minimum down payment, ideally 5%). That's 20-to-1 leverage on your money. What does this mean? That means if your property was bought for $100,000 (and you put down $5,000 for 5%), and the property increased in value by 3% in the first year, that is actually $3,000. Therefore, you just made a 60% return on your money. You put down $5,000, and at the end of the year, there was a $3,000 increase. That is AMAZING. How did you get a 60% return? Leverage. The ENTIRE property's value grew by 3%, not just your $5,000. Very few investments out there will give you that kind of leverage and return, safely and steadily year after year.

The way I view real estate is similar to owning shares in a company. If you believe it is a promising company with strong growth potential, then you buy shares in it (ie. You invest in the company). Think of real estate as shares in a city. If you believe the city has a strong growth potential, then you buy real estate in that city.

The basic steps for a rental property are as follows:

1) Acquire or Save a Down Payment

2) Ensure target property will cash flow after mortgage and expenses

3) Make offer on Property – know your numbers for maximum Purchase Price

4) Purchase Property

5) Fill with tenants

6) Collect rent

7) Refi after 1.5-2 years, repeat

Step 1, the easiest way is to save and invest until you have the minimum down payment and closing costs as well as a few months carrying costs. Carrying costs would include any expenses you would need to pay over a few month until you fill the house with tenants (Step 5). This includes mortgage payments, utilities etc. Step 2 is where you do your due diligence. Your property should be in a high demand area for home ownership, a high demand area for rent, and easily accessible by public transit. High demand areas are places with a lot of job opportunities or near post secondary institutions.

Understand the neighbourhood demographics – is this a predominantly family area, student area, young professionals, elderly or mixed. Based on the demographics, what is the market rent you can get for your property. The ideal rental property gives you both cash flow and appreciation (capital gain). However, if you have to pick one of the two you will have to assess which is better for your current situation. If you need more cash flow to achieve most of your financial goals, target cash flowing rental properties. If you have ample cash flow from your job and other ventures, your target may be more on appreciation. In this section, I will focus on cash flowing properties.

To achieve cash flow, your total gross rent needs to be greater than mortgage payments and other monthly expenses (utilities, property tax, maintenance, insurance etc). You can estimate the monthly utilities by speaking to the current owner or their realtor. The annual property taxes, you can find on the listing information about the property (divide that by 12 to estimate how much you should be putting aside monthly for the taxes). Property management usually charges up to 10% of your gross rents. Next, to calculate your monthly mortgage payment simply google

133

"mortgage calculator" and click on any of the banks' calculators that pop up. Fill in your mortgage amount and the currently mortgage rate, and the website will spit out your monthly mortgage payment. Using your monthly cash flow target, you can determine your maximum purchase price for the property.

Pretend you want to make $500/month from the property. Your total gross rent is $2000/month. All your monthly expenses are $500/month. Therefore, the maximum amount your monthly mortgage can be is $1000 if you want to hit your goal. Inputting this into the mortgage calculator should give you the total mortgage balance. Now add your down payment to the mortgage balance, and that will be your maximum target price for the property. Anything lower than that price, means you have a lower mortgage, which means more cash flow than your original target!

When you rent to tenants, your ideal tenant is a short term tenant (1 to 2 years), rather than a longer term tenant. This is because there is a law against raising the rents above approximately 2% a year (in Toronto – other areas will have a slightly different percent increase allowable). However, market rents rise much faster than 2% a year. Meaning year over year, if you have long term tenants, you will be losing money. For example, if the monthly rent is $1000, next year you can only increase the rent to $1020 per month, however, market rents might have risen to $1100 per month due to high demand (which will be the case, since we only buy property in high demand areas). This means you are losing $80 per month or almost $1000 for the year. This will happen against the next year. You will increase rents to $1040 per month, but market rents will be $1200 per month. This means you will lose $160 per month or almost $2000 for the year. That means over a two year period, you've lost a total of $3,000. Now just imagine if your tenant stayed there for 10 years! That would be a disaster. Typical long term tenants are generally retirees or those that are on benefits from the government. Shorter term tenants tend to be young professionals and growing families.

Who are the best short term tenants? University and college students! They move around from year to year, and even if they absolutely love your place, they won't stay longer than 2-3 years.

The example below is a real life example from one of my students based on my teachings (he currently has 3 rental properties, is only 21 years old and has just graduated with his Bachelors degree from the University of Toronto). The area we focused on was extremely close to a university and college. The university is growing year after year. The opportunity is that the university has over 20,000 full time students, but only 2,000 on campus beds. That creates a massive shortage, and massive demand for student rentals. Students pay rent for the entire year, but only live there for the 8 months of school. The average rent is $500 per month for a room in that area.

- Example: It is a 2 story house with 3 bedrooms (BR), 2 washrooms, and an unfinished basement, with an asking price of $325,000.

- Opportunity: Minimal renovation on the basement to add 3 bedrooms, and a washroom. Add 1 bedroom in place of the living room (the smaller the common areas, the less attractive it is for parties – therefore, less headaches and damages. Living rooms don't make money. Bedrooms do.)

- Renovation cost: $15,000

- After Renovations: 7 BR (one room on main floor converted to BR), 3 washrooms. Appraised value with finished basement, $395,000.

This is the initial investment hypothesis. Every investment you make, there needs to be a rationale as to why it will make you money. If the rationale (your hypothesis) doesn't work out, then you drop the investment and move on. Don't get attached and try to make it work.

To buy this house, we need the minimum 5% down, which is $16,250. Closing costs we can estimate at 5% which is another $16,250 (this includes land transfer tax, HST on the high ratio mortgage premium, legal fees etc). Carrying costs for the renovations (2 months): $3,000 (includes mortgage payments and other monthly expenses).

On top of that, we need $15,000 for our renovations. This is a total of $50,500 needed.

Once we are done with the renovations, we want to refinance the property to take out as much money as we can.

Currently, we have a mortgage of $308,750 (which is $325,000 the purchase price - $16,250 the down payment). When we refinance, we get a new mortgage for 80% of the property's new value of $395,000 which is $316,000. This new mortgage pays off our original mortgage of $308,750, leaving us with cash of $7,250 ($316,000 - $308,750). This cash reduces our total capital invested into the property to $43,250 ($50,500 - $7,250).

Now we want to see what our cash flow will look like. Our monthly mortgage payments will be $1,496. Our expenses consist of: Property Tax = $1500 yearly, $125/month; Property Management = $0 (for your 1st property, I recommend managing it yourself so you can learn. Once you know what is needed to manage a property, no property manager can trick you into over paying for things), Utilities = $500/month, Property Insurance: $1,350 yearly, $112.50/month, Maintenance/Labour = $150/month. Therefore your total monthly expenses are $887.50.

With 7 BR at $500 each per month, your gross monthly rent is $3500.

> Cash Flow = Gross Rental Income – Everything Else

> $3500 - $1,496 - $887.50 = $1,116.50 per month free cash flow!

That's an extra $1,116.50 every single month, which is $13,398 per year – that is amazing!

Your cash on cash return is a ratio of how much cash you generate per year compared to the amount of cash you invested.

> Cash on Cash Return per Year = Free Yearly Cash Flow / Total Invested x 100

> $13,398/$43,250 x 100 = 30.98%, which is pretty much a 31% cash on cash return.

A-M-A-Z-I-N-G! Name me one investment that will generate for you 31% cash in your pocket every year.

Your actual return is even HIGHER. Because your property will appreciate a few percent every year, and part of your mortgage payment, you are paying yourself (by paying down the debt). If we forget the mortgage repayment, and we only count the appreciation at a conservative 3% (3% of $395,000 is $11,850) then your total yearly return is much greater.

$13,398 (cash flow) + $11,850 (appreciation) = $25,248 is your total return on an original investment of $43,250. That is a HUGE 58.4% return a year. That's consistent year after year like clock work. Whoever tells you they don't like real estate is most likely broke and cannot afford to buy any (don't be like that person)!

It is not surprising that most of my students tell me that this course changed their lives! If you are looking to own more than one rental property, you need to check out www.dumbmoney.ca for how to properly structure your property portfolio to protect not only the assets but also protect your rental income from taxes.

Buying a Business

Everyone reading this has an entrepreneurial mindset. Entrepreneurs want to solve problems, you've identified that one of your problems is a lack of knowledge of how to build wealth and cash flow.

So now, you want to be an entrepreneur. You want to run your own business. Great! Now all you need to do is to think of a crazy idea that hasn't been done, learn the skills to launch it, put a team together, raise the money to pay for everything, and promote it like hell, and hope people like it! If you can do that, then you've got the next Facebook or Uber! However, you should note that 95% of new businesses and ventures fail in their first three years.

How can we be an entrepreneur while minimizing risk as we have with most things we do in this book. Minimal risk, maximum gain – that's how we build wealth.

Creating something new, different, and in demand from scratch is harder than you think. We don't need to create the next Facebook to make money – you can expand on an existing successful cash flowing business (sounds a bit like rental income from real estate doesn't it?). Currently in the market there are hundreds of healthy family run companies that have no succession planning. Many businesses are run by parents whose children want nothing to do with the business, which is unfortunate – but fortunate for us. Therefore, for these business owners, the only path forward for them to retire is to sell their business and use the proceeds to fund their retirement.

These are multimillion dollar businesses that you can buy today! Before you say, that you can't afford it – remember what we have learned. There are solutions to everything. Everything in finance is the same. To buy something, you need a down payment or equity, and then cashflow/income to support the loan or mortgage. To do so, we need to answer 3 questions:

1) How can we save enough for the down payment on a business?
2) How can we generate enough cash flow or income so that the banks will lend us several million dollars to buy the business?
3) How can we successfully run a business that we know very little about?

The answer to all three of these questions lead back to the same place. The actual business itself.

1) How can we save enough for the down payment on a business? *From the business.*
2) How can we generate enough cash flow or income so that the banks will lend us several million dollars to buy the business? *From the business!*
3) How can we successfully run a business that we know very little about? *From the business!!*

Take a moment and get a bit creative. We need to work backwards from question 3 to 1. The same with every investment decision we make. How can we minimize risk in our investment hypothesis? To run a business successfully, you need to understand every part of the business. Who best to teach you than the actual owner themselves? What is to prevent the owner from leaving the business entirely once you buy the business? How do we incentivize the owner to teach us, mentor us, and have our interests aligned?

We keep the owner as a shareholder in the business!

If it is a $5,000,000 business, we have the owner keep 30% of the business, we buy the other 70% through a bank loan. The bank loan is funded by the 70% of the business' cash flows which we now own. The owner maintaining 30% in the business provide us with the equity of the business which acts as the down payment. And because the owner owns 30%, they want to make sure the business is healthy and growing so that their 30% when you may them down is more than it is today. You can buy them out over a 5 year period, or however long you think it will take for you to learn the business.

You just bought yourself a healthy, cash flowing business which will be 100% yours in 5 years!

When you buy a business, you want to understand the industry. What factors affect industry growth and slowdowns. What happened in the last industry slowdown? A rising tide lifts all boats. If the entire industry is about to grow rapidly, then owning a business - even an average one, in that industry will be very lucrative.

Below is an example of a business I was looking at a few years ago. I decided against buying it, and I will walk you through my decision making process.

Background of the business – it is a family run manufacturing business which makes and supplies a lot of the crown moulding for houses in Canada with manufacturing and warehouses in the Ontario and British Columbia area. Asking price of $4,500,000.

Step 1 – is the industry growing or slowing down? The industry at the time was flat, but as you know, I love real estate. Job growth, population growth, technological advancements, longer life spans all contribute to a higher demand in housing. So, I believe there is value in this business long term.

Step 2 – what happened to this company the last time the industry slowed down? This happened in 2008, when the US mortgage sub-prime crisis happened. Unfortunately, this company began in 2009 when the market started to recovery. So, we have no data on how an industry down turn and affect this business.

Step 3 – analyze their financial statements. We want to see growth, or at least stability. Most business owners will get tricky and try to make their business look as good as possible when they are getting ready to sell. Don't be fooled.

BALANCE SHEET
AS AT DECEMBER 31, 2016
(Unaudited)

ASSETS

	2016	2015
CURRENT		
Cash	$ 484,778	$ 63,782
Accounts receivable	465,846	517,554
Inventories (Note 2)	655,678	977,254
Sales tax receivable	-	7,157
Prepaid expenses and deposits (Note 11)	132,684	85,288
	1,738,986	1,651,035
NON-CURRENT		
Trademarks	2,921	2,921
Accumulated amortization	2,893	2,884
	28	37
Property, plant and equipment (Note 3, Note 7)	2,142,667	2,234,284
	2,142,695	2,234,321
	$ 3,881,681	$ 3,885,356

From this balance sheet, we see that Cash has increased a lot from 2015 to 2016. Why is this? Did they sell some assets to free up cash or did they make more sales? Why a dramatic increase?

Accounts receivable means people or companies owe them money for goods. AR decreased a bit. Inventories decreased quite a bit.

What I want to draw your attention to is the Property, Plant and Equipment. This $2,142,695 plus inventory ($465,846) is your Liquidation Value. That means, if everything in the business goes wrong, these are tangible assets you can sell. Therefore, you want to have these properly appraised to make sure the market value is

142

as shown on the balance sheet. If so, this is essentially your worst case scenario.

Now for debt side of the Balance Sheet:

******* INC.
BALANCE SHEET
AS AT DECEMBER 31, 2016
(Unaudited)

LIABILITIES

	2016	2015
CURRENT		
Accounts payable and accrued liabilities	$ 476,697	$ 535,997
Customer deposits	22,303	-
Employee health tax payable	-	219
Due to related party (Note 12)	10,074	510
Sales tax payable	15,269	-
Income taxes payable	7,918	-
Due to (HOLDCO) Ontario Inc. (Note 8)	3,630,013	3,630,013
	4,162,274	4,166,739

SHAREHOLDER'S DEFICIENCY

ISSUED CAPITAL				
Authorized	Issued			
Unlimited	1,000	Common shares	10	10
DEFICIT (Note 7)			(280,603)	(281,393)
			(280,593)	(281,383)
			$ 3,881,681	$ 3,885,356

The largest glaring thing is the Deficit under shareholder. This means the owner has been taking money out of the corporation. Was this a dividend payment? A loan without repayment? Are they in some sort of financial trouble? Normally when a dividend payment is made, it is because there is a profit surplus in the company. This is not the case here.

Under Current (debts) it shows an amount of $3,630,013 owing to the Hold Co (this is generally a separate corporation that business owners create which owns their operating business. This allows dividends to pass from the operating business to the Hold corporation tax free. Remember limited liability – therefore if the operating business gets sued, only assets within the operating business is at risk. Therefore, you want to remove as many assets and/or cash as possible to the Hold Co tax free). What is this amount and what is it comprised of?

****** INC.
STATEMENT OF DEFICIT
FOR THE YEAR ENDED DECEMBER 31, 2016
(Unaudited)

	2016	2015
BALANCE - beginning of year (Note 7)	$ (281,393)	$ (168,916)
Net income (Note 7)	223,290	100,523
Dividend	(222,500)	(213,000)
BALANCE - end of year (Note 7)	$ (280,603)	$ (281,393)

Pretty much confirms what we thought – the owner has been funneling money out of the corporation into the Hold Co. As we see the Shareholder Deficiency matching the balance at the end of the year due to the dividend being paid. In 2015, we see the owner paying out more in dividends than the company actually made in net income. This is a red flag – it shows a lack of responsibility from the owner in terms of cash flow management. Not sure if this is the type of partner and or mentor we want to take on.

Income Statement:

******* INC.
STATEMENT OF INCOME
FOR THE YEAR ENDED DECEMBER 31, 2016
(Unaudited)

	2016	2015
REVENUE		
Sales	$ 4,132,752	$ 4,016,413
COST OF SALES –SEE SCHEDULE	3,097,454	3,146,060
GROSS PROFIT	1,035,298	870,353
EXPENSES		
General, sales and amortization – see schedule	562,256	559,983
Marketing and product development – see schedule	241,834	209,847
	804,090	769,830
INCOME BEFORE INCOME TAXES	231,208	100,523
Income taxes	7,918	-
NET INCOME	$ 223,290	$ 100,523

You can think of this as the company's cash flow. We see that revenue increased, while cost of sales decreased. Normally cost of sales is the cost of producing the product they are selling. Therefore, as revenue's increase, cost of sales usually increases as well. (If you sell more things, you need to build more things, therefore you cost of materials for building those things are higher since more materials means more things built means more things to sell). Everything else is fairly in line. Net income doubled due to a decrease in cost of sales and higher revenue. Why did this happen? Especially right before trying to sell the business.

At this point – we don't need to bother analyzing the business. This is a losing business to buy. Why is that you ask? The owner is asking for $4,500,000, for a net income of $200,000 (in a good year). If we move forward as planned, we need to borrow 70% which is $3,150,000 from the bank. We will own 70% of $200,000 net income which is $140,000. This means monthly we will receive $11,666 which barely enough to cover HALF of the monthly bank loan. This means we are losing cash flow every single month if we purchase this business. Now, in their BEST year, they made only

$200,000 – imagine what would happen in a bad year. This is a poor investment. Close the books and move on to the next deal.

I'll tell you a story about gut-feeling. Your gut will save you – trust your gut. There was this Niagara Estate Winery for sale for $6,000,000. It was family run, and the son had just graduated with a business degree. He was unsure of whether he wanted to run the winery or not. (Someone with a business background and full knowledge of the business not wanting to run the business – possible red flag). They had 29 acres of land, and a few wines in the LCBO. We toured the estate, sampled their wines and overall, it was a good time. They were very hospitable (but again, who wouldn't be if they were being paid $6,000,000). When it came time to looking at the numbers, that's when things got funny. The son stated, he couldn't disclose their actual numbers because wineries are a protected business. So instead, he pulled out an excel sheet he created with assumptions to run some made up numbers. He then went on to claim that China loved their wine and buy it at $xx/litre. All these sales were cash, so they don't have any documentation of it. (There is always a paper trail of the order or at least the shipping documents). Perhaps China would be a good area we can ship to, regardless of what they are currently doing as I have some strong connections out there. In any case, I said thank you and I'll think about it.

On my way home, I made a few calls to my overseas friends in the wine business and unfortunately the price the seller quoted was far too high for shipping out to China, as they had many other equivalent wine options at a far lower price point. My cousin from New Zealand was also in the winery business, so I asked her opinion. She said, "Wineries are a great way to make a small fortune as long as you started with a very big one." Essentially meaning, they are a great way to lose money if you don't know what you are doing.

Any time someone can't show you the real numbers, politely thank them, and run! Haha, obviously this was a bad deal. Months later after I had completely forgotten about them, they reached out with a much lower price point of only $4,000,000. That's a 33% price drop from the lofty $6,000,000 they were gunning for. It's obvious they were having trouble selling and wanted to get out ASAP. Trust you gut – when it says walk away, don't even bother giving it a second thought. Even with the lower price point, the gut said no.

Note: To buy a business, you need to cultivate your deal sources. Let people know what you are looking for, put the word on the street. The more businesses you can look at, the more options you have.

"You are only as good as your last deal."

Section 7: Negotiations

Throughout this book, you've learned a lot about how to manage your finances and all the opportunities out there. But to lock down these deals, you will need to negotiate them. Even if you are interviewing for your first job, the negotiation process is extremely important. A lot of times we over look the importance of our first job. However, this sets the bar for the rest of our lives. How so? Each of your promotions will be based on your last annual salary. If you start at a $40,000 annual salary compared to a $45,000 annual salary, in 10 years, that would be a big difference in your pay. Let me walk you through this – each promotion you get a raise depending on what your current pay is. Even between companies, each company understands and is fully aware of the other company's pay ranges for any particular position. Pretend that a level 1 employee has a pay range of $40,000 - $45,000. If you jump in and accept $40,000, this is how your future will look. If every promotion is a 10% pay increase, and every 2 years you are promoted, in your 1st two years you will be paid $40,000; 2nd two years $44,000; 3rd two years $48,400; 4th two years $53,240, in the last two years $58,564. In 10 years, that's a total income of $488,408. Now, if your starting salary was $45,000 instead and we use all the same conditions, in 10 years your total income will be $549,459. That is a difference of $61,051! Over 20 years, that's a $159,374.20 difference, if you invested this money and it grew over the 20 years, that's even more money you just lost.

In the following section I will walk you through how I structured the negotiation for my promotion from consultant to director at Investors Group. I achieved this promotion in only 18 months from the date of my hire. Head office regulations dictates a minimum of 2 years in the consultant role along with other criteria before being considered for a promotion to director. Most consultants take an average of 5 to 8 years before being promoted to the director role.

However, through a proper negotiations, I was able to get the head office exceptions I needed to move up in only 18 months. The fastest promotions in the history of Investors Group from after implementing the 2 year policy.

Every negotiation is an information gathering session. The more information you have, the better you can frame your point of view. Ideally, you want to leave the negotiations with a commitment from the other party that they will follow through on. Therefore, you cannot bully the other side into agreeing with you, because the minute they leave the room, they will renege on the agreement and/or never do business with you again.

I have read multiple negotiation books and have taken bits and pieces from each of them and applied the concepts in my own deal making. The below is my summarization of the steps I follow when I structure my negotiations.

1) Set the atmosphere
2) Seek out information
3) Label negative emotions
4) Allow them the opportunity to say No
5) Summarize the conversation
6) Define what is Fair

When you sit down for a negotiation, you want to be in a neutral comfortable location. You want to guide the other party down the path you want. To do so, you will be using subtle nudges. You don't want the other party to be distracted at any point in the negotiations because if they miss a few of your nudges you may fail in your negotiation process. You want to sit with your back to the wall. Your face is the only thing the other party should see. The last thing you want is for the other party to start looking past you to the cars and people outside the window. Make sure your back is to the most boring thing in the room, making you the most interesting thing they can look at.

In any negotiations process, it is highly advantageous to understand the other party. To do so, you need to extract as much information as possible. This is the base on which you will build the beginnings of your negotiations around. Make sure your foundation is sound. To extract information, you want to use a process called mirroring. Basically, all you do during the conversation is repeat the last 3-5 words the other party said in the form of a question. When you feel as though you have enough information to move on, then do so. Until then – continue mirroring. It may seem unnatural at first, but the other party won't notice. Just mirror and wait. The other party will want to fill in the gap of silence and provide you with more information. We are raised to want to be polite and accommodating, therefore the other party will feel uneasy leaving a gap in the conversation.

Next, we want to bring up any obstacles you sense may be there. We want to label any negative emotions or feelings. Use phrases such as "It seems like …", or "It sounds like …" etc. You are attempting to summarize your understanding of the mirroring data gathering.

Once we have enough information, we want to use this to create an open, welcoming atmosphere that will encourage a candid honest conversation. How do we do that? We want the other party to say no to us. That seems counter-productive at first, however, saying "no" triggers something in our minds that allows us to open up more. As we spoke about above, we want to be accommodating and agreeable, therefore it is only when we are comfortable with someone that we can be our true selves. It is only when we are comfortable with someone that we can say no. Therefore, by allowing the other party the ability to say "no" to us, we are triggering their brain to tell them that they are in a safe environment. But we want to guide the no's. What we don't want is "Can I have a promotion?", "No!" That's the last thing we want. We want to guide them down the path in which when they say no, it is really a yes, because we are asking them inverted questions. "Do you believe there is someone else more qualified for the position?" A "no" reply to this question is a yes to you achieving what you want. What you want to do here, is build a "No ladder." This is opposite to what untrained sales people try to do, as they often try to build a "Yes ladder." You will notice that you and others do the same thing when it comes to annoying people building a yes ladder. You just agree with them so they will stop bothering you and go away. This is NOT what you want to do. You want to build a "No ladder" which does two things: 1) create an open conversation, and 2) guide them towards your objective through inverted questions.

A lot of times, during this portion of the negotiation some unanswered questions may arise – if you need to, don't hesitate to go back to mirroring.

At this point, we want to summarize the conversation according to our understanding now that we have uncovered and addressed all the obstacles. This is the point we want to hear yes. These Yeses will be true yeses of agreement. We want to summarize and get a "that's right". Once we have come to a common understanding, we want to define and frame ours and the other party's actions moving forward. We do so, by labelling what is "fair." We all want to be fair. To be unfair means you are a bad person, and no one consciously wants to be a bad person. Use phrases such as "Is it fair to say that if I … then you …" By doing so we are able to frame the situation moving forward as to what both sides can expect of each other.

The below is a prime example of how I used my knowledge of negotiations to get a 100 plus year old, 8.2 billion dollar organization to change their policies for me. If you know anything about big corporations, almost everything is "set in stone," and the one thing they are not, is flexible. Fortunately for you, you are on a path greater than you, and greater than the corporation.

Graduating from my MBA at Schulich, I had plenty of opportunities for a 6-figure plus fulltime salary. However, I needed to do my own thing and make my own path. After having a taste of entrepreneurship (I built a start up during my MBA), I felt I couldn't work for someone any longer. You can imagine the push back I got from Cherie (who was my girlfriend at the time) as she wanted to get married and start a family. A cushy six figure regular salary would sure come in handy for family planning. But if you are going to bet on anything, bet on yourself. And that is exactly what I did.

I took a role as a consultant at Investors Group. This is a 100% commission based job, which means, if you don't sell you don't get paid. Which is great for the company, as they risk nothing to hire you. If you don't perform, you are broke and will voluntarily leave the consulting role and find a salary job. If you are successful, then the company benefits.

For any negotiations, you want to set the framework from the beginning. In my very first interview with the regional director, I asked for the requirements to become a director. He printed off a two page list of requirements all consultants need to complete before being eligible to become director. The items included sales goals, additional educational requirements, and a minimum two year tenure as a consultant. He also wanted to point out that most consultants don't become directors for a good 5 to 8 years. To which I said that's fine, and that I would be taking the consultant position (before I was offered it) because I fully intended to be director in the minimum 2 year time frame.

In my first full year as a consultant I generated over six figures in commission income (which is far better than a salary since you can control your own tax rates) which was unheard of from anyone starting in the company, fresh out of school. I was the top 5 out of all new consultants under 4 years in the business, and top 100 across all consultants in the country. (Investors Group has well over 5000 consultants across Canada). (This was due to my advanced knowledge of financial strategies which allowed me to out advise all the bankers and senior advisors in my path, allowing me to win over their current and potential clients. To win, you need to understand what your industry is lacking, and offer that.)

At this point, I invited my regional director to brunch, as it was he, who had a large say in whether I move up to director or not. I was about 15 months into my role as a consultant. We went out to the local Coras which was down the street from the office. I came early, picked a booth, and sat with my back towards the wall.

When we arrived, we had some light conversation, ordered, and then it was all business. I pulled out the 2 page directors' requirement sheet, in which I had completed and gone beyond the basic requirements in record time, except for being a consultant for 2 years. My goal for the negotiations was to get his commitment to make me a director once my two year anniversary hit.

We began to discuss the director position, at which time I began mirroring. Him – "The director position involves many more responsibilities than the consultant role." Me – "more responsibilities..?" etc. During our conversation, and through my mirroring, a consistent theme arose. He felt I didn't have enough experience with the company to make an effective director.

I combined "labeling" and "forcing the no's" together with the phrase, "it seems like you feel I may not be ready to handle the role of a director, do you feel that someone else is more suited to the role?" To which he replied "No, I think you would make a strong director but you haven't been with the company long enough." I continued to guide him along the No ladder with inverted questions.

I moved on to defining what is fair. I started with "Would you say that the company is undergoing quite a few major changes and we need a director with a track record of performing to help push these new initiatives?" To this, he agreed. "Would you say that I have exceeded the expectations for a consultant at any level, new or senior?" To this, I already knew the answer as the stats across the company showed I outperformed. To this, he agreed as well. "I greatly respect you as a business man who looks to increase the pie through mutual partnerships, would it be fair to say that if I continue to perform as I do, I've earned the role of director?" (I embedded another technique of flattery, in which you label the other person, to which they will want to live up to). To this he agreed that was fair, but I had one more obstacle, the largest one, to overcome. "That would be fair, but Mitch, you need to understand the decision to make you a director is not mine to make. It's head office." You will come across this often, mostly in the form of "Sorry, I can't make that decision, I need to ask my wife/husband." You can easily overcome this by isolating the outside party which is not involved in the conversation. I replied, "I see you as a mentor and attribute a good portion of my success here to your guidance and leadership, I cannot influence or control what happens at head office, what I am asking for is your support, and only your support. Would it be fair to say that I have your support and you will fight for me to be a director as long as I perform as we have agreed?"

By isolating him from head office, I won his support which places a lot of weigh at the head office level. Rather than waiting for the full two years, I officially become a director only 18 months from my start date as a consultant.

The basic framework for the negotiations shouldn't be antagonistic. You are not enemies looking to conquer one another.

You are allies on the same team, trying to solve a mutual problem. Always give the other party the illusion of control by asking them for their suggestions. "How would you like me to proceed?", "How can we solve the issue here together?"

When it comes to numbers, you want to re-anchor the other party. For example, if you know the pay band for your job is between $40,000 to $45,000, then HR probably thinks that by offering you $43,000 is generous. However, when you state your ideal salary, you will want to be well above the top line limit. Your ideal salary should be $47,258 annually. This accomplishes two things. Firstly, it re-anchors them towards the upper limit of the pay range as now the proposed $43,000 seems quite low. Secondly, by providing an odd number, they will automatically assume there was some sort of reason for that particular, exact number. This makes your request more reasonable because they assumed that there is some validity to it. (And vice versa if you want a lower number, re-anchor lower).

When they try to negotiation you down, build another no ladder. "That's a very generous offer, but I'm afraid I cannot accept that." "I'm sorry, I just can't do that." "I need to be a responsible steward of my resources." Never say no flat out. Always shift the decision making reasoning to something else. (ie. I need to ask my spouse – just say it in a more sophisticated way).

Note: Remember the keys to a negotiation, i) Collect information, ii) Make the other person validate themselves, iii) Anchor, iv) Define metrics for success, v) Give them the illusion of control (make them offer suggestions)

"Be the hero of your own story."

Section 8: Becoming The Go-To Person

This will be extremely important in the life of your career. This is the difference between being offered opportunities versus hunting for opportunities. You need to be top of mind. You need to be the hero of your own story.

To do so, takes some preparation and planning. Building your reputation so that people know you before even meeting you is key. Therefore, you need to know and cultivate yourself into the person you want other people to speak about.

Have a clear understand of who you want to be and how you want to be known. As we spoke about before, the clearer this "future you" is, the easier it will be to fill in the gaps of what you need to do and/or accomplish to become this person. Have the goal in mind, and work backwards. To impress upon you the importance of this, imagine me asking you to walk in a straight line. Every now and then, I will randomly place a chair, a wall, a car in your way. What will you do every time I place something in front of you? Sit down? Stop? Go back to where you started? Now, what happens if I ask you to walk in a straight line from here to the farthest wall in the room you are in and I randomly place obstacles in your way? Most likely, you will go around or over them, because you are well aware of your final destination and you understand what you need to do to get there.

This is the same as understanding who we want to be, who our future selves will be. Having the final destination in mind will simplify your decision making and which opportunities you should accept and decline.

To separate yourself from everyone else, you need to be willing to do what others won't. At times, there will be opportunities to get involved in projects at work, in which no one on your team will want to do. This is usually because people on average don't want to stray too much out of their comfort zone, as they are scared to fail. For us, this is the perfect opportunity for us to differentiate ourselves from the masses. We see this as an opportunity to gain additional skill sets and networks within the company. A lot of times, new projects involve outside departments or teams allowing you to increase your workplace visibility. The more people who know you, the more people who work with you, the more people will speak about you, the more top of mind you will be.

Don't be scared to take on a project which is outside of your wheel house or area of expertise. As we spoke about before, be that 10% to 20% ready, and find mentors and resources within the company to guide you the other 80% to 90% of the way. These mentors and resources will usually be more senior managers in the company. These mentors and resources will later become advocates and allies for you, making it easier for you to move up in the company and or pursue other projects. As Richard Branson says, "Say yes and figure out how to do it after."

If you look at professional athletes, the ones that put in the time and the work during team practices and alone, are the ones that excel and become the stars of their team. This concept is called "First on, Last off." First to come to practice, last to leave practice. This will not only hone your skills, but visually, your managers and teammates will be aware of your presence. This does NOT mean, hanging out by the coffee machine all day so you are always around. That's the opposite effect you want. If you are there, it is because you are providing value. You need to be visibly performing, not visibly goofing off.

There is a fine line between performing at too high a level that you can never be promoted compared to performing well enough to be promoted. This is particularly obvious in a sales position, as sales teams have targets they need to hit, and as long as the team hits the targets, then the manager good look. If you are the main sales earner for your entire team, you've pretty much guaranteed that you will never be promoted. Why is that? That's because your manager cannot afford to lose you, as you are the only reason why your manager looks good and is hitting the team's sales targets. Understanding how the company works, and what the success metrics look like at the higher levels will give you a guide on how you should perform. The more powerful allies you have, the easier it will be for you to move. This is particularly useful if you are a star and your manager can't afford to lose you. Larger more powerful managers are known to poach members from other teams. Having several more prominent senior managers bid for you will greatly increase your value (supply and demand).

In business, there is a saying, "You are only as good as your last deal." The way I see this, is that everyone has a spotlight on them which is brighter or dimmer relative to someone else. You want your spotlight to be the brightest in the room. The result of this, is that you will be the easiest one to spot, thus making you top of mind. Every time you complete a task successfully and or close a deal, then your spotlight shines brighter. It will stay bright until someone else's is brighter than yours when they complete a task or close a deal equal to or larger than yours.

To keep your spotlight bright, you want to keep taking on opportunities and closing deals that come to you while your spotlight is bright. While your spotlight is bright, don't get complacent and relax. Now is the time to absolutely kill it. Now is the time when opportunities and deals will be dropped on your lap because you are top of mind. Take the ones that will make your spotlight shine even brighter. Rinse and repeat.

Combine this with developing your human capital. Make sure you are growing into the future you. Don't rest until you grow into that person. Remember just because you are resting doesn't mean everyone else is. If you rest, while everyone is sprinting – then they

160

will soon overtake and be well ahead of you. In the world of finance, everything is relative. When you have more purchasing power than everyone else, then you are wealthier than they are. If everyone has $10,000,000 in their bank account – that becomes the new average, and all the stores and product prices will rise to reflect that. It is the same as the laws of nature, we are all running as fast as we can to keep up with everything else. As the rabbit is running faster to outpace the fox; the fox is running faster to catch the rabbit.

Run fast; Run smart; Run straight through anything in your way! See you at the top!

"If I have seen further it is only by standing on the shoulders of giants."

- Sir Isaac Newton

Final Thoughts

Reading the this to completion and understanding the concepts is but your first step. Bruce Lee said it best, "Knowing is not enough, one must do." That is now your responsibility. You have no excuse not to take taken, unless you give yourself one. It easy for us to be satisfied and stop here because it's "enough." Anything can be enough if we rationalize it enough.

There was a story I heard once about a farmer and his friend. The friend came over to the farmer's house one evening for dinner and to catch up on old times. Over the course of the even, the farmer's dog, who was laying in the corner, would randomly yelp every 10 to 15 mins. At the end of the night, the friend couldn't contain his curiosity anymore and asked, "why does your dog yelp for no reason?" The farmer said, "Oh, that's because he is laying on a sharp nail." To which the friend replied, "why doesn't he just move?" And the farmer said matter-of-factly, "because it doesn't hurt enough."

Don't wait for the pain – work now, work smart. You've already done the boring stuff – you've read the book. Now go out there and action it!

Go to www.dumbmoney.ca, register for the wealth building course once you've completed it you will be eligible to connect with me one of one to pick my mind about your financial plan, access your different opportunities etc.; download the excel files; and join the private Facebook group and connect with me. (To access only the financial planning excel sheets, email me at mitch@dumbmoney.ca)

As part of the online wealth building course, I've included my infamous "Retire in 10 years making $10,000 per month residual income lecture" which requires you to hold down an entry level job paying $45,000 annually. Several of my students from the

University of Toronto have already started to implement this and are on track to retire in their early 30s. Also, how to get started in development (condos, townhouses etc.) and much more!

Coming soon to www.dumbmoney.ca, is the Dumb Money: Day Trading course – how I am able to grow my portfolio several percent weekly consistently.

Warmest regards,

Mitchell (Mitch) Huynh, B.Sc., B.Comm., M.B.A.

10073854R00092

Manufactured by
Amazon.ca
Bolton, ON